RESTLESS TEENS

Train up a child in the way he should go
[and in keeping with his individual gift or bent],
and when he is old he will not depart from it.

Proverbs 22:6, *Amplified Bible*

KEN STOLTZFUS

RESTLESS TEENS

and those who nurture them

On the interaction between
grownups, and teenagers
who are forging
their own identity.

© July 2008 Ken Stoltzfus, GoodBooks4Me, Ltd.
All rights reserved. No part of this publication may be reproduced, stored in a retrieval system or transmitted, in any form, or by any means, electronic, mechanical, photocopying, recording, or otherwise, without the prior permission of the publishers.

ISBN 13: 978-0-9818638-0-1
ISBN 10: 0-9818638-0-9

printed with pleasure at:
Carlisle Printing
OF WALNUT CREEK Ltd.
2673 Township Road 421
Sugarcreek, Ohio 44681

If not available from your local supplier, additional books may be purchased wholesale or retail from:

May be purchased for $5 each, postpaid in the U.S. Please mail check or money order to:

Ken Stoltzfus
P.O. Box 228, Kidron, OH 44636

RESTLESS TEENS may be read, and downloaded free at www.john2031.com/books/rt/main.html

See www.john2031.com for more inspirational resources

Cover and Text/Interior Design: Nic Miller

Scripture taken from the HOLY BIBLE, NEW INTERNATIONAL VERSION®. Copyright © 1973, 1978, 1984 International Bible Society. Used by permission of Zondervan. All rights reserved.
The "NIV" and "New International Version" trademarks are registered in the United States Patent and Trademark Office by International Bible Society. Use of either trademark requires the permission of International Bible Society.

Dedication

I dedicate this effort to today's teens everywhere who struggle to emerge into their own personhood in the midst of the sometimes unhelpful expectations of Christian institutions. By God's design their deepest craving is to know Him, followed by their need to become the specific individual whom He created them to be. We can make it so hard for them in spite of our best intentions.

Secondly, I dedicate this book to those of my high school classmates, and to others of my generation, who because of the dynamics described herein have struggled these many years to feel and enjoy the love of God. But there is still hope. More later!

Commendations for
Restless Teens

Dr. Noah Martin
Founder, New Day, Inc., Johnstown, PA

This book will open your heart and mind to see restless teens in a different light. Ken knows what it means to be a restless teen, and his subsequent lifetime of experience and observation provides rich insight and guidance for those who nurture today's youth.

Society may call them "troubled kids" or "at-risk teens," but Ken will help you experience our restless youth in a more positive way. *Restless Teens* offers many suggestions for working with teens who are often misunderstood and thus misdisciplined. Parents, teachers, pastors, youth directors, school administrators, the juvenile court system, and others will benefit from this book. Knowledge is often the beginning of change and sometimes a little understanding will go a long way. Nurturing them may not be as difficult as it seems!

Noah Martin, D.Min., is founder of New Day, Inc., a Christian ministry to at-risk youth and their families in western PA. Dr. Martin is an ordained minister in the Church of the Brethren, has published several books, and was a high school classmate of the author.

Paul G. Leaman

Principal, Eastern Mennonite School, Harrisonburg, VA

Ken hits the nail on the head when he describes the challenges many "restless teens" face within organizational structures because of our traditions and patterns that do not match the inner workings of their soul. These youth may be more prevalent than keepers of the status quo prefer, but they are masterful at teaching us patience, forcing policy review, and puzzling the significant adults in their life. By God's remarkable grace and personal resilience, they frequently grow up to become significant leaders in, and philanthropic supporters of, our churches and charitable organizations.

The proverbial phrase, "You can't fit a square peg into a round hole," is an accurate analogy for many of these youth. In theory, educators know that instructional differentiation for meeting the individual needs of students is a requirement for any master teacher and administrator. Unfortunately, theory often falls short in our practices. The restless teen needs personal awareness, and educators would be wise to find creative and customized ways to dote positive attention on their most challenging students.

Ken's heart is to help us nurture today's youth so that more will bless our world tomorrow. He masterfully describes the oft misunderstood teen from the context of personal experience, and offers a grandfather's perspective for adults in the trenches who find themselves frustrated by what we perceive to be a teen's spirit of rebellion. Ken offers ideas and God's grace to help youth workers discover God's hope in every person—even the restless ones.

Paul G. Lehman earned a B.S. in Biology Education at Eastern Mennonite University, and an M.Ed. degree from James Madison University and has ten years experience in teaching and school administration.

Pastor Nathan Ward
Senior Pastor, Wooster Church of the Nazarene

I highly recommend *Restless Teens*. I have read widely and must say that this is one of the finest books I have ever seen on the topic of influencing teenagers as they navigate their way into adulthood. This material is relevant and full of challenging, practical truths that desperately need to be applied. Every adult who deals with teenagers ought to read, absorb, and refer to this book.

Serving as a full-time youth pastor for 16 years in three churches was a tremendous learning and growing experience. The longer I served teens, the more I grew to love them as I saw their hearts and their unlimited potential. I cannot think of an exception. When properly understood, teens really are easy to love.

Over the years there were many tough situations to deal with, but I came to the realization that most kids labeled as "bad" were actually "good kids" who had been severely wounded. Most were injured in their closest and most trusted relationships, unintentionally or otherwise.

Because I love teens, it is my heart's desire that they be understood and heard. This is a necessary part of the process of their becoming all that God has created them to be. I deeply appreciate resources that give adults greater insight into teenagers . . . and into themselves, enabling them to make a more positive and intentional contribution to our youth.

Since 1995 Nathan Ward has been Senior Pastor of Wooster Church of the Nazarene, a dynamic and growing church of 1500 in Wooster, OH. A graduate of Mount Vernon Nazarene University, Pastor Ward is a mentor in the Pastors of Excellence program of Ashland Theological Seminary.

Acknowledgments

This book exists only because of the encouragement and thought-provoking observations and comments of many who contributed to it.

There were six "first responders" who affirmed and commented on an initial crude attempt at expressing these thoughts, thus spurring me on. They were, in order: my twin, Karl, with whom I share concern for today's kids who are like we were in 1958; son Mark, a deep thinker about life and relationships; Ken Weaver, a friend and bold Christian; Dr. Noah Martin, my high school senior class president who invested much of his life helping at-risk kids and their families; Ray Nethery, pastor to pastors, mentor to me for many years, and one who has modeled an oft-evasive blend of boldness and kindness which I so deeply covet; and Ben Smith, former youth pastor, and now a banker whose love for God inspires me.

Two Christian ministry leaders joined the effort in a significant way. Pastor Nathan Ward of Wooster Church of the Nazarene was a youth pastor for 16 years and now senior pastor since 1995. He's the most pastoral person I've ever met, and there's not much about people that is hidden from him. I take it seriously when my pastor says something like, "You're on the right track, Ken. Go for it." And Paul Leaman, Principal of Eastern Mennonite School in Harrisonburg, VA understands and loves the kind of teens I write about. His many suggested additions and deletions enriched the material so much.

A brief, casual conversation with aircraft maintenance guru Matt Near led to the material on influence versus control. Steve Flack, former pastor and one who reaches toward restless teens, encouraged me and provided some key thoughts. And many other informal exchanges provided seed which grew into what I think you will find to be stimulating concepts and principles.

Beth Feia, former book editor turned full-time mom, contributed immensely by reviewing an initial rough draft and giving me some sober advice on what works and what doesn't. I needed that. Marcus Wengerd and Nic Miller of Carlisle Printing offered valuable guidance on title, cover design, and other finishing details.

Finally, my wife Elaine reviewed and proofread several manuscripts, asked helpful questions, and tolerated a lot of "I'll be in my study for a while" as I wrote. Her support is indispensable, both in loving me these many years as one of the kind of person I write about, and through the process of expressing that on paper. Guys like me need a wife like Elaine—and I am among the most fortunate of men.

Contents

Preface

Part one   The Challenge of the Teen

1. Crackers in My Soup 3
2. The Few 7
3. Invisible, Odorless—and Deadly 11
4. Is It Rebellion?........................ 15
5. The Mandate 19
6. I Watched.............................. 25
7. Our Response 29
8. Attitude Says It All 31

Part two   The Challenge of the Institution

9. The Christian Institution and Its Rules 37
10. Authority and Rules for a Reason......... 41
11. The Abuse of Power 45
12. The Christian Educator 49
13. When Adults Fail 51
14. "God Help the Little Ones!" 55

Part three   For Adults Only

15. Three Fingers Pointing Back............. 61
16. The Dark Side of Power 67
17. God's Way Versus Satan's Way 73
18. So, Which Is It?....................... 77

Part four   Helping Restless Teens
                                         Understand Themselves

19. We Value Them for the Person They Are .. 83
20. They Have Predictable Vulnerabilities..... 85
21. They Will Have Some Social Challenges... 89
22. There Are Keys to Their Success.......... 91

Part five	**Wrapping It Up**
23	The Battle Is the Lord's................95
24	The Flight Instructor 99
Conclusion	105

Part six	**Afterwords**
A	RestCAT.............................112
B	Public or Christian Education?..........113
C	"God Help the Grownups" 114
D	Potential Risks with Adoption 117
E	The Few as Adults.....................119
F	The Heart and Hand of God............121

The Final Word

Preface

Restlessness in teens as they advance into their personal identity and adulthood is as normal as the sunrise. However, the process can be a perplexing blend of wonderfully rewarding and indescribably painful experiences for both teens and those who nurture them.

This book considers how adult rules and boundaries can affect the development of our teens, and especially those who think "outside of the box," as we say. It is an attempt to express concern in an area of the nurturing process which is not often addressed, but it is not a comprehensive treatise on raising teens.

When I write that teens want authority in their lives, but that it needs to be from one who respects and values them for the individual they are, it comes from the deepest part of my inner being. I've felt and observed enough to understand those incredible youth who become confused about themselves, human authorities, and God—because of tensions they experience in Christian institutions.

All I have ever done was shaped by a life philosophy built upon II Cor. 3:18, which speaks of "*being* transformed." A sometimes overwhelming sense of personal weakness has been balanced by the confident hope that as I continue to walk with God, He will further instruct, correct, and purify me. Please keep that in mind as you read this book. It's a good thing if God challenges you through this material, but please view it as "moving on with Jesus" and not a negative or condemning thing.

This material can give you a new perspective on your teens and help you guide them into the unique person that God created them to be. You can do so much to support them and to minimize the potentially damaging effect of the concerns raised here. Portions of this book can be a mentoring tool as you walk alongside them through the rough terrain of those years.

A few adult readers will gain insight into how their own lives were handicapped decades ago by dynamics described here. Please dare to advance into new levels of freedom and joy in knowing and accepting yourself in a deeper way. I wish you well in that pilgrimage!

One factor I've struggled with in this book is the relationship between typical restless teens, and those I refer to as "The Few." The Few are an important subpart of the teen family and need special consideration, but the principles that apply to understanding them also relate to most teens—albeit to a lesser degree. And who can say exactly where the line falls between the typical teen in pursuit of personal identity, and The Few? It is also true that when we place excessive expectations upon typical teens, we can drive them toward the kind of response we would expect from The Few! Please apply what I'm trying to express, in varying degrees to specific individuals you are in relationship with, and forbear my sometimes awkward attempt to span the range of teens we're considering. Thank you!

And I must add this. I am told by professionals who have previewed this material that little has been written on this topic from the viewpoint of being an advocate for teens. My writing is not based on training and research, but on nearly seven decades of a mixture of blunders and successes in making my way through life as one who identifies with the kids I describe here. Take it for what it's worth. Agree or disagree. Cut it up, refine it, do some research, and write a more professional book—but please don't ignore it. We can't afford that.

Ken Stoltzfus

part one

The Challenge of the Teen

1	Crackers in My Soup
2	The Few
3	Invisible, Odorless—and Deadly
4	Is It Rebellion?
5	The Mandate
6	I Watched
7	Our Response
8	Attitude Says It All

We'll start by looking at teens themselves and move toward some of our responses to their youthful zeal as they pursue their personal identity. In the process we'll consider the responsibility God has given us toward them and will try to understand why we sometimes respond in counterproductive ways.

chapter one

Crackers in My Soup

The concepts that teens form about themselves, God, and life are substantially based on their experience in the home, church, and school. The ways in which we express authority, and the tools we use toward that end, affect them for life. This is serious business!

When I was a child we weren't allowed to break crackers in our soup. "It isn't proper" was all the reason we were supposed to need. We may have winced as we watched other kids crush those saltines into their tomato soup, but the rule was the rule. Certainly their families didn't understand what it meant to be proper.

Then I married Elaine. She was well-mannered in general, but she broke crackers in her soup! There was some tension in our home over the matter.

Several years later we moved to New England, where I worked as an orderly in a hospital. A professor from the University of Vermont was a patient there for quite a while and we became friends. It was the beginning of a pilgrimage.

As Professor and I talked he would occasionally ask, "Why do you say that?" Until then I hadn't thought of such a question very often. You see, at least back then, "Just because" or "Because I said so" was assumed by adults to be enough reason for us to believe something or obey a rule. They were the adults, we were the children, and what they said was to be final. There wasn't much need for us to think, and our questioning something they said was not a good thing. It is an approach to life that can follow one into adulthood.

By this time we had a son who was old enough to want to break crackers in his soup like other kids did, and Elaine didn't see it as such an awful thing. Following Professor's approach, I thought into the matter and decided to redefine "proper" for our family. Trivial as it may seem, it was the beginning of a personal pilgrimage which continues to this day. The simple pleasure of breaking crackers in my soup was only a small part of the benefits to come!

New England was followed by six months in aircraft mechanics school in Oklahoma. The church we attended there introduced us to a refreshing approach to the Christian life. Their focus was more on an inner relationship with God than on rules to control outward behavior.

Following two more years in the family aviation business in Pennsylvania, we went to college in Virginia. The greatest benefit for me was not the college-knowledge and a business degree, but the mindset of inquiry as a way of life—the value of asking, "Why?"

I would hasten to say that I value etiquette at the table. And I have tried to live a principle-based life in my own spiritual walk, in family and other relationships, and in ministry, business, and various aviation activities. Be assured that I hold firmly to the historic, core absolutes of the Christian faith. But I have grown into a freedom to ask "Why?" and to do things differently if there was reason to—and no good reason not to. As I told a grandchild at a recent family gathering when she was losing a friendly argument with a sibling, one mark of growing up is the freedom to change one's mind about something!

We know that by their early teens our youth are on a quest to form their own identities. Much has been written on this normal process of discovering who they are as individuals and how they relate to God and society. It is a time when they sort through beliefs and values around them and choose their own. Matters such as honesty, timeliness, emotional expression, the value of others, respect for the law, the place of money and possessions in one's life, their attitude toward alcohol and drugs, the implications of gender, sexuality, and marriage—and where God and His Word fit into all of that.

Parents and church and school leaders watch anxiously as our youth cycle back and forth between appearing to accept and then reject the beliefs and values we have tried to communicate. We so badly want them to follow us. We truly believe we know what is best for them! It's so hard for us to plant and water the seed, and then release them to God and trust His process of bringing it to life. Our natural tendency is to make and enforce rules to keep them moving in the right direction. Something like a cattle chute.

I share the concern. However, my sense is that our heavy application of rules at this stage in their life is potentially counterproductive. Giving our youth mandates to be unthinkingly accepted and blindly obeyed may not be the best thing.

A pry bar can be a tool or a weapon, depending on how and why we use it. It's the same with rules. It might be good to ask ourselves: "Are our rules and boundaries tools to disciple and mentor our youth, or weapons to control them?" If the former, we will be much more comfortable with their asking, "Why?" In fact, we will welcome questions because they give us an opportunity to impart information and values to them.

And there's another benefit. This approach will shape the spirit in which we both create and enforce rules. It will compel us to assure they are practical and that their purpose is to communicate principles and values, and to maintain social order. We will feel more obligated to be fair and consistent in how we enforce them if they are mentoring tools rather than weapons of control. We will be more inclined to correct and nurture, rather than only punish, when they are violated. And, recognizing the way in which the typical teen responds to them, we will create the least number of rules necessary to achieve our objectives.

Don't we *want* our youth to become "thinking" adults? Don't we want them to develop their own values for life instead of just trying to fulfill someone else's expectations? And can't we do that more effectively by creating a constructive mentoring environment to influence them, rather then trying to control them?

We shouldn't be surprised if our teens react negatively to control as they move through the years of developing their own identity and values. We may have forced them to resist us as they express a deep, inner, God-given drive to become their own "person." And it is especially so with a certain group of teens!

chapter two

The Few

There will always be a few teens who more than others will push against boundaries and appear to struggle with authority. A common but false assumption is that they are rebellious at heart.

Society needs a variety of personalities and gifts in order to function well. God has made it so. We need the more naturally compliant, and institutional leaders love them. For the most part they are satisfied with things as they are. But we also need those who "push the edges," always restless with boundaries. It is at the core of their being, and sometimes they drive those in authority crazy. They are "The Few, the Brave, the Misunderstood."

These are the teens who are more likely than the conformist to change their world in years to come. They will invent, create new art forms, architectural styles, technologies, and countless products and innovative ways of doing things. They are the ones who will find a previously uncharted path to the mountain peak. And they will become the founders of businesses, churches, and ministries.

They won't accept, "It can't be done." They will be brave risk takers, daring to go where others fear to tread. They may fail more than others, but only because they take more risks. For now though, The Few are frequently misunderstood and misjudged, a situation that is furthered by the fact that they are often bold in expressing themselves.

Usually such a teen doesn't understand himself and why others respond as they do. Only by mid-life will some recognize that their life-theme has been something like the Ralph Waldo Emerson quote on my office wall: "Do not follow where the path may lead. Go instead where there is no path, and leave a trail." Others *never* figure that out and live a lifetime of feeling like a misfit.

Many older and wiser church and school leaders know that the teens they had the most problems with "back then," are time and again the ones who contribute the most to our institutions twenty or more years later—*if* they survived those earlier years and remained connected. That's true, and a twinge of sadness in having misjudged them could empower these wiser leaders to help today's parents and institutional leaders respond to teens in more constructive and supportive ways. It's never too late to do the right thing. This ought to speak volumes to our current, younger leaders, especially those who have not raised teens themselves, and more than that, teens of the more rambunctious type.

Because these restless and questioning kids are misunderstood and viewed as a behavioral threat, they may be ostracized by adults, further confusing them about who they are. We are responsible to give them a place among us and to help them grow in self-understanding. They need to feel cherished and valued, not just tolerated, in the home, school, and church. They need and seek adult approval even when they hold us at arm's length as they attempt to gain their personal identity. Believe it or not, they really do want to please us and to be accepted by us. Everyone gets hurt when we are unable to recognize and respect them for their God-given gift, and help them grow into all of the potential that He has placed within them.

Some restless teens will be outwardly aggressive, others less so depending on personality and life experiences. The response of adults around them has a lot to do with how aggressive they need to act in order to express themselves. My observation is that boys are often more aggressive than girls, but that either gender can be an "out of the box" type of person. Either can be confused about themselves and handicapped in their growth if not properly recognized and mentored.

We can love our children passionately but still hinder them if we don't understand them. In fact, love and good intentions without understanding will work against us. Our deep love and concern can cause us to try to control them and to protect them in ways that are unwise. What they *need* is love, understanding, acceptance, and active mentoring. A good self-test might be to check our spontaneous response when they do something that concerns us. When our mind and emotions leap in response, is it to control them or to better understand them?

One of the obstacles we adults face is recognizing the shortcomings of our own attitudes. We need a willingness to search our soul, and attempt to understand the teen's perspective. But don't we often feel the problem is theirs? And don't we like to believe we are right as the adult? Please don't let that discourage you. Don't stop here—these kids need us too badly!

Each personality has its predictable downside, which if ignored will diminish the individual's contribution to

The Challenge of the Teen

society. By understanding, affirming, and nurturing these teens we will not only minimize the potentially negative side of their personality, but we can help them blossom into all that God intends for them. As they come to know themselves, and even to enjoy being who they are, they will enrich *us* too, making it a win-win situation.

These are wonderful, delightful kids. We would enjoy them a great deal more if we were strong enough not to be threatened by them, and if we could allow ourselves to value their place among us. It is realistic to be optimistic about their future. Even those like my favorite cartoon character who, despite a non-endearing moment, has a ton of energy and potential to offer the world. Let's never allow ourselves to squelch the Hammies whom God places under our care.

© www.babyblues.com, Aug. 10, 2007, used by permission

In this book we'll talk a lot about the Hammies among us, but we'll also consider the larger picture of restless teens as they try to figure themselves out in a world of complex and sometimes seemingly contradictory expectations of human authorities, God, and their inner "person." And we'll try to understand why we feel so challenged by them, and why we so easily default to control in our response. But first, let me tell you what I mean by "control."

chapter three

Invisible, Odorless— and Deadly

Friends were flying from Kansas to Ohio one cold night several years ago. A daughter complained of feeling sick, and then lost consciousness. She had been sleeping with her head against the side of the aircraft.

The father contacted Air Traffic Control and declared an emergency, which gave him priority on the airways and at the airport. He was cleared to land at Indianapolis and was given the taxiway location where EMS would be waiting for them. The EMTs were at the cabin door before he had the aircraft shut down.

They administered oxygen to the girl and took her to the hospital. Her dad suspected that the problem was carbon monoxide poisoning from the aircraft heater. When she was sufficiently recovered they continued their flight to Ohio—wrapped in blankets instead of using the heater. An investigation revealed that the heater canister was cracked, allowing carbon monoxide to enter the aircraft cabin. The victim had been sitting with her head almost directly over the hot air duct. Carbon monoxide is invisible, odorless— and deadly. The end result could have been much worse.

Sometimes we describe a person as being "controlling," meaning that they tell others what to do, and like to have their own way. I'm suggesting that some people are just bossy, while others are actually controlling. And I'm going to say that "control" is like carbon monoxide. It is invisible, odorless—and deadly. For both, there are warning signs for those familiar with and alert to them, but they are easily missed. Because of its invisible and odorless nature, control is hard to define, but because it is so deadly we must attempt to.

Control, as the word is used here, is when we usurp the free will of another. We override their personhood and subjugate them to our expectations. There is usually a mixture of self-serving interest and, at least the appearance of, concern for the welfare of the one being controlled. Control is rooted in pride, in effect declaring ourselves superior to the other. It often, but not always, occurs when one exercises a rightful authority toward the other, but uses it differently than its intended purpose. We are often ignorant of what we are actually doing, and many who control would deny it.

I have been on both sides of control enough to know how it feels. I know how it felt for another to loom over my personhood, trying to move me in the way that served his interests while thinking he was acting out of concern for my welfare. And in a certain way he was, but it was absolutely crushing to my personhood. In the 1960s I was in a very secure place in life professionally and financially, but could not move in the direction of God's plan for me. By His grace and power, and with Elaine's courageous support, I was able to break away, even though it meant taking her and our three young children into a vast unknown. Over the years I've been able to encourage others who were being diminished in a similar way.

In 1982 I started an aircraft parts business with our sons. Christian family businesses had been a keen interest of mine for years. I had observed many—a few good ones, numerous otherwise, and thought I knew how to make it work.

However, a couple of years into it things started to go sour. There was growing conflict among us. I had so much pain in my gut that I thought I was getting an ulcer. I pled with God to tell me why it hurt so bad to work with my sons whom I loved so much. This was to be "a dream come true!" One day He answered me and it wasn't flattering.

We'd had a disastrous fire four months after we started, and God had used me in a significant way to lead our family through a recovery. We were a young business, very much in debt because of the fire, and were still defining and establishing ourselves in the marketplace. We needed clear leadership! I had a Bachelor's Degree in Business Administration/Management and many years' experience in the aircraft parts business. I was President and General Manager too. And my sons, "kids" so to speak, with little experience and no college, were frequently challenging my policies and expectations. It was very easy for me to fall into the "Father knows best" mindset.

What God spoke to my heart was simply, "The problem is that you are controlling your sons just like your father controlled you." That hurt deeply, but I knew it was true. My father was a good man and a good father in many important ways. But he, like countless others, including some who will read this book, didn't understand what "control" was. He wasn't aware of its foundational motive or the impact it had upon another. In spite of the fact that I had earlier felt deep pain in the process of being controlled, I was now doing the very same thing to my sons! I really *did* care about them personally, and about the business, but the way in which I was going about it was too much control rather than influence. It was more "over" than "alongside." It was odorless and invisible, but deadly. Sometimes soul-searching regarding our own pain can help us understand the pain we are causing others.

Determined to break that generational pattern in our family, I "declared an emergency," as it were. I repented of it and stepped out of ownership and the place of power in the business. I offered to work for our sons as an employee or to find a job elsewhere. They asked me to do their marketing, which I did for many years. It was a relationship which allowed me to contribute meaningfully to the business through marketing—and by influence from alongside—and because of their generosity I had considerable time for ministry, including mission work in East Africa.

Control is insidious, that is, subtle in manner and sinister in effect. All who practice control will struggle to acknowledge it within themselves and to repent of it, but not everyone needs to take the drastic action that I did. It was a costly step, but few have experienced a father-son relationship as enjoyable and fruitful as I have. I was able to establish the foundational principles which the business is built upon, and then because I am more the founder type than a long-term builder, my sons did a better job of building it than I could have!

A properly functioning aircraft heater is a blessing on a cold day, but a faulty one is deadly. Godly leadership is needed in the home, church, school, and business, and is life-giving, but control is as potentially dangerous as a cracked aircraft heater canister. We'll talk more about that in Part III, "For Adults Only," but first, some more thoughts on The Few.

chapter four

Is It Rebellion?

The response of The Few to authority and boundaries is not initially rebellion. Please believe that. We need to understand that they view boundaries differently than others. They are always alert to a better way of doing things. Boundaries are not an authority issue for them as much as a potential obstacle to something better. By their God-given nature they are uncomfortable with things as they are. They get cerebral claustrophobia if they are not given room to question, explore, and test.

While many adults analyze life from what is inside the boundaries, these youth might almost "live" on the other side, viewing life from what they can imagine to be there. They can "see" things before they actually exist. And isn't it true that most "new" things were at one time on the other side of then-present boundaries, and that the only way to discover and develop them was for someone to cross those boundaries? And didn't that usually make some folks uncomfortable?

These nonconformist teens will identify flaws and weaknesses around them, not because they are critical, but because they see how things *are,* relative to how they could be—and they have the courage to say that. They will be fearless because of the value they see "on the other side," not because they are arrogant and think they know best about everything. That trait can follow them through life.

Some walls, then, are hard for The Few to accept and respect because to them they are not only ill-designed or implemented, they are a hindrance to better things. To others they may be walls of stone but to them they are papier-mâché. They are not authentic and need not be taken seriously.

Their incessant questions and challenges are not questioning and challenging us personally as much as the way we do things. However, their challenge of our ways of doing things presses against the traditions, rules, and power structures that have made us comfortable. Regardless of intent, it is often taken personally by those in power, and especially so if the teen does not communicate the kind of respect that the adult requires.

These youth are observers and thinkers. They respond to the "just because" or "because I said so" kinds of answer in the same way a balloon does when we try to squeeze it in our hand. It simply bulges out in a different place. The parallel is as painful to consider as it is unavoidable, when we remember that the balloon pops when we squeeze it too hard.

In a rules or authority-driven environment such as some Fundamentalist and conservative Evangelical circles, The Few may determine to experience life in what they consider a larger or more authentic way than what they see around them. By rules or authority-driven I mean the mindset where rules and authority are an "end" in themselves, rather than tools to help us achieve an end. They are upheld regardless of how practical or equitably enforced they are, or how they impact the quest of the teen heart.

It is not uncommon for Christians to find our spiritual

security in our beliefs, customs, and rules. In an uncanny way these can usurp a vital relationship with God through Jesus Christ as the basis for our assurance of salvation. We feel threatened, then, when our youth don't embrace them—judging or at least assuming that they are thereby rejecting God. This is a delicate issue. There are several possible ways to respond as their searching questions challenge us to be honest about the integrity of our basis for spiritual security. Some parents and church leaders don't really want their youth to "think" and to question—they just want them to obey.

Further, some like to quote Ephesians 6:1-3 about children obeying their parents, but forget about v4, *"Fathers, do not exasperate your children; instead, bring them up in the training and instruction of the Lord."* I take *"of the Lord"* to be a very significant part of that verse.

Somehow we need to be humble and wise enough to search our hearts and make sure that we are drawing the lines with humility, wisdom, and integrity, and in places that really matter. It is a desperately weak argument to insist that teens are "rebellious," and especially to declare that they are rebelling against God, when they challenge legalism, spiritual shallowness, or traditions which are not truly life-giving.

The challenges of our youth become a major crisis to adults who misinterpret what is taking place. Many are not realistic about the God-given process of the typical teen moving into appropriate independence, and they understand The Few even less.

I'm not saying that all teens who have a problem with rules and boundaries are among The Few. Some are simply resisting the efforts of parents or others who seem to be thwarting their advancement into independence. Others are described in the next chapter. But among our teens are these whom God has created to be the more outward-looking ones. Far too often we miss what is happening and end up diminishing them. Or worse.

My twin brother, Karl, proposes that Christian schools give all jr. high or high school students a personality profile test. When issues arise, the administrator would go to the student's file and see how "normal" the student is acting in relation to his or her personality and other factors. It could give many clues on how to respond to and mentor them. Obviously teachers would need some orientation to personality types, and someone on staff should be more thoroughly trained. What an incredible investment that would be!

Karl's idea inspired me to push the concept out to something I'll call the "Restless Child Analysis Tool." RestCAT would consist of a series of questions to assist in evaluating the student and figuring out why they act as they do. *

*Please see Afterwords A: "Restless Child Analysis Tool."

chapter five

The Mandate

Train up a child in the way he should go [and in keeping with his individual gift or bent], and when he is old he will not depart from it.
                    Prov. 22:6, *Amplified Bible*

Fulfillment, for all of us, is found in becoming the individual whom God created us to be. Frustration comes when that is thwarted.

The promise in Proverbs 22:6 is for those who train a child in the way that *he or she* should go; that is, in accordance with the unique person that God has created each one to become. Each child is unique. No generics. The mold is thrown away each time one is made.

Parents or other authorities sometimes err by trying to form a child into something different from God's plan. We want them to fulfill *our* expectations, i.e. business, ministry, sports, music, or one of many other interests. In most cases it is an honorable thing, but it might not be what is "inside" the child. When Elaine's and my three sons were in their teens, we said we would support them in any honorable occupation they chose. That included areas well outside of our personal skills and interests. We expected them to learn good work habits and basic mechanical skills, and to embrace the discipline of doing things well, but otherwise the field was wide open to them.

To start with, the term "my child" is a misnomer of sorts. Soak on Psalm 139:13-16 a few moments and consider how deeply God has vested Himself in each child. *"For You formed my inward parts; You wove me in my mother's womb. I will give thanks to You, for I am fearfully and wonderfully made; Wonderful are Your works, and my soul knows it very well. My frame was not hidden from You, when I was made in secret, and skillfully wrought in the depths of the earth; Your eyes have seen my unformed substance; And in Your book were written all the days that were ordained for me, when as yet there was not one of them."*

To be given a child to rear for Him is a sacred trust. We are responsible to do our best to nurture him or her into the specific individual that God intends. When we entrust them to the church or Christian school we are responsible to assure that they share this vision.

We certainly agree that God has created each of us uniquely through the blending of gender, personality, physique, learning styles, cognitive abilities, and more. We also know that each individual is influenced and shaped by that person's environment. A dairy farmer knows that cattle need to be treated individually—how much more so for young adults!

There are many reasons why we can miss this point for our teens. Some parents and educators appear to have a cookie-cutter view of children. They respond as though all children are alike, trying to teach and raise them identically and mistakenly expecting similar results.

There may be cultural issues too. My father's interest in airplanes simply wasn't the right thing for a young

Mennonite man in the mid 1930s, and he faced a lot of negative response from the church community. Fortunately, he was strong enough to persevere and to become a superior pilot and a pioneer crop duster in the East. He proved himself enough to earn the respect of his family and of the aviation community around the world, but the rejection he experienced as a young man made it hard for him to be comfortable with the institutional church for many years.

Further, we can handicap our children because of our own narrow range of interests. If we're into things of a mechanical nature like auto repair or a machine shop, our child's interest in music can throw us a curve. An entrepreneur might gasp at the thought of his son or daughter becoming a social worker. Our interest or disinterest in sports can shape how we respond to a child who is gifted, or not gifted, in that way.

If our parents kept us in a "small world," there can be a subconscious tendency to keep our children in a small world. We can practice an unspoken, "If I couldn't spread out and become the person that was in my heart, you can't either."

We might be jealous of the potentials we see in our children, maybe even abilities that could help them become what we could have been if we had been encouraged to—or even *allowed* to. How different it would be if adults would bless children in going beyond themselves in every possible way, including spiritual vitality, range of interests, education, skills and abilities, financial stability, a vibrant marriage, and more. It lies within parents, educators, and church leaders to encourage and equip them in those ways, i.e. to believe in them and help them appropriately believe in themselves. There is no reason why that can't and shouldn't happen in many areas of life, especially if we are humble enough to let them learn from our mistakes. I propose that seeing our children go beyond us is one of the greatest joys a parent can have—and one of the greatest marks of our own success! If the Biblical principle of sowing and reaping is true, there will be a harvest and all will benefit.

Especially if our child is among The Few and we are of the more compliant type, we can try to shut them down when we see them "pushing the edges" *too* much. Some parents obviously forget their own teen years as they succumb to the definition of supposed normalcy and the demands of living within the confines of religious, cultural, or institutional expectations.

It is true that we adults can interfere with God's creative design of our teens when we limit them with our boundaries. These are only some of the ways in which well-intentioned parents and others diminish their young people. And maybe even now, years or decades later, some need to go back and acknowledge to their adult children the failure to bless them into becoming the person that God had put within them.

There are three things we should remember in addition to the Biblical mandate of Proverbs 22:6. First, we should consider the words of Jesus in Mark 9:42* regarding how serious it is to be a stumbling block to the little ones. Millstones are not nice neck ornaments. Secondly, we should remember that Colossians 3:20* is followed by v21*. Lastly, there is little in life that equals the joy of vesting oneself in others, seeing them succeed, and hearing God whisper "well done" in your ear. It's more than worth the effort!

If at any point in this book you feel that I'm overstating my case and that I'm overly sympathetic toward teens, please pause to reflect on studies which indicate that well over half of our present teens will exit the church by their early twenties. Some say over 75%. Look at your own church over the past ten years, and do some Internet research. We need to do something differently!

* Please see "The Final Word" at the end of the book for all of the Scriptures which are referenced throughout the text.

chapter six

I Watched

I watched Charles (names are changed) struggle through his high school junior and senior years. He was considered by most to be a kind and respectful young man and I experienced him as such.

Charles was an adventurous, six-foot, strong, "big world" guy, but his Christian school had a rules-driven, legalistic culture. It was like stuffing him into a two-foot-square by five-foot-tall box and closing the lid. It's no wonder that the sides of the box bulged!

I saw in him a rich, God-given potential. The kind of heart that explores; that is not satisfied with the status quo; and yes, that pushes and sometimes crosses the boundary lines. He had that creative, innovative spirit which is so useful in our world and in the Kingdom of God, and the kind of strength that can prevail through the tough spots. And there was a look in his eye. He had a quiet confidence, a sense of who he was or could become, and something that kept him just a bit "at arm's length" in a certain way. It said, "I am Charles and no man will dominate my spirit." I liked what I saw.

Some in authority, however, saw the same look and misinterpreted it. It infuriated them because they took it personally as defiance of their authority, and they determined to control his person. He was singled out for special scrutiny and was disciplined for things that others got by with.

When we don't accept, affirm, and nurture teens like Charles, we in effect force them to push through our resistance and move out on their own, compelling them to learn from their own mistakes. We shouldn't be surprised if they begin to dabble in areas of life that are off-limits to a Christian, but we ought to humbly review the path that got them there. Sometimes their failure reflects our own more than we'd like to think.

I watched Becky too. A fairly quiet, intelligent freshman who had some of the same characteristics as Charles. Her personal strength and resolve, and an ability to challenge, could be part of a brave new world in some way. As Charles, she had a tender spirit toward God.

Becky is the kind of gal who could some day express the heart and hands of God in a war zone or deep in the bush. And as she went she would most likely see and implement more effective ways of doing things.

Predictably she wrestled with boundaries, especially the inequitably applied ones she saw around her. And she was offended by a teacher who berated students in the classroom. She expressed that and became a target of the teacher who now determined to make her submit. It was an outrage to me that following a series of supposed infractions she would be sentenced to solitary confinement (okay, in-school suspension) for a whole school day.

People simply couldn't understand why Becky and a friend ran away one night shortly thereafter. Fortunately, it turned out okay with nothing worse than indescribable anguish and fearful imagination on the part of her family and friends as they searched a nearby stream, woods, and warehouse, and scoured the rural roadways late into the night. A phone call brought an end to the search just as several sheriff deputies were interviewing parents and gathering the information and photos needed to launch an Amber Alert, and nothing was hurt except a whole lot of pride.

Sad, isn't it? I wish these were isolated examples. Are they?

How could these things happen—and especially in a Christian school? It's simply because Charles and Becky are among "The Few, the Brave, the Misunderstood." Those who misunderstood them, and for whom they refused to kowtow, were determined to force them into submission. They didn't stop to consider whether their approach was godly, or to weigh the impact it would have upon the student's personal development. The relationship became power-based and they had the power.

We would be amazed by how little understanding, acceptance, and affirmation of their personhood it would take to reduce a teen's aggressiveness and help him or her become more at ease. They are driven by their need to find and prove themselves, and our wise and humble response could make it so much easier for them—and for ourselves.

chapter seven

Our Response

Sometimes teens' inquisitive nature and constant testing of the walls around them is offensive because those in authority are personally satisfied with the present walls. They can't imagine the need for something better, and it is especially so if they created the walls themselves. Other leaders feel a need to protect their authority, viewing any imagined infringement as a power issue. They are attuned to possible challenges with an almost hair-trigger mentality.

A frequent response from parents and school or church leaders is to judge the child as rebellious. Predictably, the next step is to "lay down the law" to try to force them to conform and to stay in the sterile and safe little box that has been created for them and their peers. The assumption is that everything would be fine if they would just obey rules and respect grownups.

The individual personality of the student and the influence of their home, school, and church cultures contribute to what follows. Some teens are strong enough to tough it out. Others learn to play the game and put their toes on but not across the line. Some are sly enough to get by with crossing the line. A few have parents with enough power to intimidate those in authority and "cover" for the child. To our shame some teens abandon who they were meant to be and simply bow to the pressure to conform.

Too many become horribly mixed up about themselves and crash under the load of confusion and guilt. And then we wonder why kids run away, become truly rebellious, slide into depression, or take their own life! Is it possibly because they are being told that the person God has made them to be is not acceptable to us? Consider the crushing burden this puts upon such young people, a burden that is even heavier for Christian teens because they are made to believe that they are unacceptable to God!

The need is to understand, respect, affirm, and bless the person he or she is at the core, and to nurture that person into healthy expression. We need to help these teens to understand themselves and why they respond to boundaries as they do. *Only then* can we help them learn to live harmoniously within reasonable boundaries and how to cope with seemingly unreasonable ones.

Let me take you back to the spring of 1956, when I attended a Christian high school. Mennonite, conservative, lots of rules. My restlessness with all of that was at least equal to our Charles and Becky, yet I could take you to the place on the sidewalk between the dorm and the Administration building where I met "Brother Weaver" (Amos Weaver) that morning. Principal, pastor, kindly but serious, and all the trimmings (or lack thereof) of conservative dress. I had been invited to his office more than once. Yet as we passed he gave me a knowing smile. A smile that said, "Yes, Ken, you're the restless type and you cause us a lot of grief at times, but I know your kind and you're going to turn out all right." That went deep. Why do I feel it like it was yesterday?

chapter eight
Attitude Says It All

Authority empowers one to fulfill a responsibility already given. When this power is used to fulfill the responsibility, it is generally life-giving. Even kids who test boundaries can appreciate the need for that, but when it is used differently they will find it harder to respect.

Some adults hold their authority in a firm grip, assuring themselves and others that it is immediately available. And then there are those who hold it loosely or even just keep it nearby. It is accessible when needed, but in the meantime their hand can wave a friendly "Hi!" to a teen, or be placed on a shoulder in an act of kindness. The kids know who is who!

There is something crucial at the core of how this all shakes down. Authority can be position-based or relationship-based. Teens will find it much easier to accept relational authority than strictly positional authority. And they truly do want authority in their lives—but from those who respect them as individuals created in the image of God. They respond more positively to those who see a "person" inside of them, and who view authority as a sacred trust to be used for their welfare.

These young people know exactly how we feel toward them, and they can't be fooled about how a given adult uses authority. A person in power who truly respects them, who cares about them as individuals, and who has a heart to help them mature; will predictably be more relationship-driven than position-driven. When authority needs to be expressed, it will be in a spirit that the kids are more inclined to respect.

One of my sons recounts the day he and some friends put shaving cream under a classroom door. The teacher simply wiped it off and didn't say a word, but he also balanced relational and positional authority in a healthy way. When he needed to draw the line, he did, and they respected him for it. For what it's worth, they *liked* him too.

The Few will be especially alert to what they consider to be hypocrisy, injustice, or inappropriately expressed authority. When Becky was doing her in-school suspension, another teacher came into the room, commanded her to stand up, scrutinized her from head to toe, and insisted that certain things didn't conform to dress code. The alleged infractions were comparable to what other students were wearing. Why did she feel the need to do that to a young person who was already being chastised, and what do you think it did for Becky's respect for authority? And what do you think it did for her self-image? Before we come down too hard on our teens we ought to ask ourselves if we are giving them reason to respond as they do.

Obviously there are many more students than teachers and administrators. And a Christian school is an educational facility, not a daycare center or reform school. We can't divert an unfair amount of time and effort toward a few rambunctious students. But please reconsider if you were preparing that argument. What these kids need most is attitude, not time. They need humble teachers and administrators who are interested in them personally, who understand and respect them, and who are committed to their growth into the individual God has created them to be. It's an attitude. It's not that hard and the reward for such a commitment is out of this world!

Aren't we quick to assume that problems between teens and us adults are because of *their* attitudes? Yes, many of them do have attitude issues, but please be honest about the fact that *we* usually set the tone for relationships. How different could things be if we were honest and humble enough to model the kind of respect and attitude that we require of them?

part two

The Challenge of the Institution

9	The Christian Institution and Its Rules
10	Authority and Rules for a Reason
11	The Abuse of Power
12	The Christian Educator
13	When Adults Fail
14	"God Help the Little Ones!"

The word "institution" suggests something that is established and which functions according to certain rules. The home, school, and church are all important institutions. If their rules and boundaries represent and communicate values and are truly life-giving, they can serve teens well as they advance into their own identity. However, it's as normal as hunger for teens to test institutional rules! They *want* to know which are valid, and we need to give them time and freedom to learn that.

The next several chapters consider how the ways in which authority is expressed in Christian institutions affect our teens.

chapter nine

The Christian Institution and Its Rules

Elaine and I and our children and grandchildren have benefited from nearly 130 years of Christian education* and 200 years of membership in the church. I'm deeply grateful for that, but have observed that there is something especially tricky about Christian institutions and their rules.

Because we are "Christian," it is easy for parents and administrators to give rules and their enforcement an inappropriate spiritual weight, regardless of the logic or effectiveness of the rules, or the way in which they are enforced. Young people who challenge or disobey the rules, or those who enforce them, are soon perceived as challenging or disobeying God. Please read that again!

This is a risky scenario. Yes, it is true that youth need to learn to submit to authority over them. And those who can't accept human authority will find it harder to accept the authority of God and His Word. However, this approach is latent with potential abuse. It can blind leaders to their humanity and the measure in which they don't accurately represent God.

How faithfully *do* our rules and boundaries in the home, church, and school represent the heart of God and support our objective of mentoring our youth into becoming followers of Jesus? And which ones have about as much wisdom and eternal impact as breaking crackers in our soup?

We can become pharisaical more quickly than we realize, being satisfied with trying to shape the outside, i.e. the appearance, instead of the heart and character. Character is more an expression of the heart than is the outward appearance, yet we so easily prefer the latter.

These are formative years for teens. I say confidently that this situation has been more responsible than we want to admit, for causing young people to become marginalized in their Christian faith. I cringe at the thought of how many develop a warped sense of, and an embittered spirit toward, God and *His* rules because of the way in which we represented ourselves and our rules to correspond to Him. That applies to the rules themselves and to the way in which they are applied.

We give our teens a distorted definition of God and then we wonder why they don't want it! They have responded, "If this is how God is—if this is what the Church is—I'll just keep my distance." They *do* keep their distance, and some for a lifetime.

Some youth walk away from God; others only leave the church. While we might insist they are walking away from God, thus vindicating ourselves in a certain way, they often aren't. Frankly, I think there are going to be some surprises when we get to heaven and see who's there and who's not.

The more spiritual weight we give to our rules and authority, the more closely we connect them to God Himself. And the more likely we are to impart a warped image of Him to our youth. That realization ought to cause the knees of some parents and Christian leaders to buckle.

We also need to be careful that our personal affirmation of teens is not conditional upon their meeting our expectations. If they experience *us* as inseparable from expectations which they view as superficial or hypocritical, and which are hard for them to respect, they can easily slide into disrespecting us personally as well.

These principles are especially true of The Few, but apply to a wide range of teens who are searching for truth and authenticity as they develop their own spiritual identity in the process of advancing into adulthood.

* Please see Afterwords B: "Public or Christian Education?"

chapter ten

Authority and Rules for a Reason

Every social group has a culture made up of beliefs, norms, ways of doing things, and more. It is an aroma of sorts which permeates the institution—defining us and creating expectations.

We construct an authority culture in our institution either by design or by default. In a school, for example, the culture established by the board can tell the administration and staff how and why to express authority. Or we can simply let it emerge in the style of the present head administrator or others without being deliberate about it.

Our rules and boundaries must be purpose-driven, understandable, practical, and equitably enforced. I was talking with a school administrator one day about tattoos and body piercing. He was revising their dress code to forbid both. I asked why he wouldn't insert the word "visible" there. People put those things in really strange places, and I felt that short of an unlikely procedure to assure that they were nowhere present on a student's body, he was writing an unenforceable rule that would dilute the integrity of the dress code in general. His disagreement revealed something about the authority culture he embraced.

If you consider the practical intention of such a rule, it is to forbid the *display* of such bodily embellishments. It seems to me that to go beyond that is heavy-handed and serves no purpose other than to flaunt one's authority and dare our youth to disobey it. My personal taste and bias do not support tattoos and piercings, but I also want to be real-life in terms of rules. And I would want to avoid the aroma of authoritarianism.

Christian schools need a dress code as part of creating a healthy environment and communicating values. However, we can write one which is not well defined, allowing it to be interpreted differently by various parents, students, and teachers. And we can permit it to be enforced more or less carefully upon certain students.

A friend told me about his granddaughter who was repeatedly called down for her skirt length. Yes, she was the restless type and from a family of only average means. The family took photos to the board showing other girls in shorter skirts, but they refused to look at them. Those girls were from families who had the kind of resources that the board valued. Things were "going downhill fast" in the girl's attitude and the family wisely moved her to a public school. She is doing well, but what do you think this kind of event told her about what it means to be godly, and how did it affect her appreciation for rules and authority?

It is common knowledge in some Christian schools that certain teens can get by with hair styles, clothing, and accessories that other students are called down for. A more active teen who questions a dress code, even an illogical or inequitably enforced one, may be held to a stricter adherence to it, being disciplined for things that others get by with. It is part of those with power showing the student who is in charge. That's not why we have rules!

Consider the case where a teacher who rarely uses pop quizzes gave a heavily weighted one on senior skip day. It took the valedictorian honor away from a senior who was a class leader, and model student and athlete, and gave it to a junior who had enough credits to graduate but was not a member of that class. What godly, principle-based objective could that achieve? What does a situation like that reveal about the school's authority culture? The administrator supported the action, but fortunately there was enough righteous indignation expressed from alongside to have the authentic honors student reinstated.

Consider also rules which are created in reaction to a specific event but which are unnecessary in a general way. For example, let's say that some students "overdid it" in their senior pranks. We can react and forbid future senior pranks altogether. Or we can *respond* in a corrective but mentoring way. We can set some defined and practical boundaries such as: "nothing destructive of property, dangerous, or disrespectful of others—and if you make a mess you clean it up by the end of the next day." Is it possible to use something like this as a mentoring situation, helping them to understand the need to use good judgment and to accept responsibility for their actions?

Please let the kids be kids sometimes. Really, how harmful *is* it if they buy some cheap clocks and hide them here and there in the school with the alarm set to go off at a certain time? Or if they "fork" the lawn, or - - ! Wouldn't it be more fun for everyone, with absolutely no compromise to our educational and spiritual goals, if we learned to smile more and didn't take ourselves so seriously! If you can't get past the "let the kids be kids" thing, you can certainly recall other situations where broad-sweeping school, family, or church rules were written in reaction to a specific event.

How would *you* respond to the following scenario at a high school graduation? A senior's name is called for him to come receive his diploma. Nothing. The name is called again. Still nothing. People are getting restless. As parents and other authorities anxiously search the auditorium, the sound of a Volkswagen engine is heard behind the stage. The curtains part and a Beetle emerges with the student behind the wheel and a (properly attired) female classmate draped across the hood holding a beach umbrella. He was called and he came, but not in the expected manner. (Their class had a beach theme for the event. The driver had convinced the custodian the night before to be in cahoots with him and to allow him to sneak the VW in.)

Fortunately the school principal was a good sport. The students got their diplomas and the custodian kept his job, but how would you or your school have responded—or *reacted*?

An aside to consider is that our authority culture is a mentoring tool, teaching students what authority means and how they ought to use it when they are in power.

chapter eleven

The Abuse of Power

A risk of over-spiritualizing authority and rules is that leaders are vulnerable to using power to cover their personal insecurities and weaknesses and to protect themselves from scrutiny and challenge.

A high school teacher can berate students in the classroom, but when one of The Few quietly goes "grrrrrr," only one of them is held accountable. The student is punished for being disrespectful and the teacher is affirmed for requiring respect. Do you sense something "out of joint" in that scenario?

Who should be held to the higher standard, the student or the teacher? Who is responsible to model the Christian lifestyle?

Sometimes those in power refuse to acknowledge weakness and to apologize because they fear losing respect and authority. Every honest adult knows the feeling, and the temptation to "save face," but we forget how much respect we earn and what a powerful mentoring tool it is when we humble ourselves and allow our youth to see us as "real!"

Teens measure their respect for parents and other authorities on the basis of who we *are*, not who we pretend to be or say we are. They *know*! Further, our actions, including what we do when our humanity shows through in some way, tell them more about God and Christianity than any amount of teaching and disciplining. To their credit they may want something better than what they are seeing in the adults over them.

When those in authority use position to protect themselves against a teen's legitimate challenge, a downward spiral may begin. Each reacts to the other with increasing intensity and soon the teen is in trouble. Too often power overrules justice. It shouldn't surprise us when this fosters disrespect in the teen toward rules and authority, and it puts a lot of responsibility on leaders to search their own hearts when conflicts arise.

If the student is a Christian, it can become a spiritual matter and a sense of guilt may follow. It would not be unusual for depression to come into such a scenario, especially in a person with a tender spirit toward God and who really wants to do the right thing. "I don't understand who I am, and nobody else does either. When I am 'me,' I am smacked down and declared rebellious. I'm confused. Those in authority over me don't like the person I am. I must be awful."

Such youth now appear to be rebellious and may be branded as such. Because of the way in which their God-given inner person is being trampled, they might actually become that.

Do we sometimes make it difficult for a teen to respectfully but candidly challenge the actions of an adult whom they feel is at fault? Do we sometimes shut them down until they are so filled with anger that they explode, and then we punish them for *that*?

Do we sometimes quickly default to, "The child just needs to learn to obey and to respect authority," as a way of dealing with conflict instead of approaching things in a team/partnership spirit?

Would you agree that we need more adults who are offended by evil in the church and our society and who can express that in a healthy way? If so, our teens response to perceived wrongs or injustice in the institution gives adults an excellent opportunity to mentor them in how to handle anger in a constructive way!

In discussing this book with a friend, he asked, "Why do we allow an adult to express immaturity or even childishness in the way they relate to teens, such as by showing favoritism, or being defensive or vindictive—but then we require the teens to respond to them in a mature way?" He continued, "If Christian school leadership truly wants to see revival, they ought to consider calling teachers and administrators to repentance for their attitudes and actions—and the students will follow." Wow—I wish I had thought of that one myself!

How often would our conflict with teens come out better if we adults were more committed to understanding their need and to responding in a mature and godly way?

chapter twelve

The Christian Educator

I know that serving in a Christian school can be a tough assignment. Teachers are frequently underpaid and may need to work with limited educational resources. They are often subjected to conflicting expectations from parents and churches in a way they would avoid in a public school. But doesn't one who chooses to serve in a Christian school accept the responsibility to be a role model and to actively nurture students not only intellectually but in their walk with God? Isn't that what we say Christian education is about?

When a restless teen meets a teacher or administrator in the hallway, the teen can "read" the adult by his or her countenance and the look in their eyes. The face and eyes can communicate acceptance and respect, but if the adult feels hostility toward or is in a power struggle with the student, it will show in a heartbeat. Either way, they are communicating an expectation to the student, who will usually respond accordingly. Isn't it challenging to all of us, even as adults, to be confronted or corrected by an authority whom we sense doesn't really care about us as an individual? And don't we quickly respond in a positive way toward one who is warm toward us, and especially those who seem to value us as a person?

A Christian teacher chooses to respond in one of several ways to a student who points out a mistake on the board. If they are insecure they may be defensive and find occasion to retaliate against the student such as in grading, dress code violations, or other supposed infractions of rules. On the other hand, they can smile, say "Thank you," and move on. Aren't they responsible to do that? And what if they were even strong enough to compliment the student? Wow!

If there has been an adversarial relationship between the student and teacher, the student might point out the mistake in an inappropriate tone of voice, creating an opportunity for the teacher to charge him or her with "disrespect." However, if the teacher is personally secure enough to rise to the occasion, she will refuse to engage the student at that level. She can, in a moment, disarm that spirit of communication and create a model for constructive future exchanges. It takes two to fight, and isn't the more mature one responsible to take the lead?

Some teachers and administrators can only maintain order by laying down many rigidly enforced rules. Their main goal is obedience; their main tool is fear. And then there is the one in authority who doesn't seem to have much problem, even without using a heavy hand. What is the basic difference? Would you agree it is because the students respect him and don't want to disappoint him? And why do they respect him? Would you agree it is because they know that he respects them as individuals, cares for them, and is trying to help them advance? Try asking some teens about that!

Isn't it this kind of modeling and nurturing that makes the extra cost and effort of Christian education a good investment for us? And couldn't this be the kind of thing that makes the difference for a student who is "on the edge" and can tilt either way in his or her attitude toward God and the church?

chapter thirteen

When Adults Fail

Parents are the teens' nurturers and protectors, but life isn't always fair and kids need to learn that. Sometimes we must let them get pushed around a bit to toughen their skin. We don't rush in and defend them every time there's some little injustice.

One thing our youth need to learn is that good people do bad things. Well-intentioned people make mistakes. Those in authority over them will sometimes act in a hurtful way. That's the way life is and we need to decide what we're going to do about it. Will we let it make us bitter and vengeful, or will we rise above it, roll with the punches and press on, becoming wiser and more mature through it? This is an opportunity for them to learn that adversity can create the setting for character development.

However, parents shouldn't "cover" insecure leaders or make excuses for inappropriate or unjust actions, especially *patterns* of offense. Please be honest about what's taking place and help the child sort it out. Allow them to candidly identify the ways in which the adult's attitudes or actions are wrong and/or hurtful.

You can't fool kids. They will see through a parent's denial of what's happening. However, here's one place where they are more like God than we adults often are. One of my sayings for life is: "God doesn't require us to be perfect, but He does require us to be sincere and humble." That is, to sincerely press toward Christlikeness and to humbly acknowledge when we fail. Kids have the same expectation! They don't expect adults to be perfect, but they do expect us to be real. They don't reject us and our authority so much because we are imperfect as because of what they sense to be hypocrisy. And isn't that how Jesus responded to folks—and doesn't that make them like Him?

When things are overtly unjust it may be time for parental intervention. "Way back when," one of my sons squealed his tires in the school parking lot and it probably wasn't the first time. He was forbidden to park at the school and had to go downtown, about a half mile away. It was a long walk, but that was fine with me. You play, you pay. However, the administrator crossed the line when another guy did the same thing and was allowed to park at a church much closer to the school. I went in, clarified that I properly understood the situation, and told him that "fair's fair." He decided that it was okay for both to park at the church.

If there's a pattern of offense at school, the parents could have the child write out a list of specifics. Some teens would be strong enough to face the offending adult themselves. In other cases the parent and child would talk about it, and then one or both would go to the school administrator and possibly to the board to express concerns.

Parents would be amazed at what it would do to the insides of a restless child when they defended them in the right way at the right time. I know—my father did it for me once. And be assured that at times just talking it out and feeling the parent's understanding and support would eliminate the need to even go to the offender!

Would you agree that sometimes adults in authority disqualify themselves from deserving respect on the basis of their actions or relationships? In this case parents should help their teens see the need to respect the offending adults for their position, and hopefully for their virtues, while not requiring respect in the same way they would respond to someone who has actually earned it.

chapter fourteen

"God Help the Little Ones!"

We know that children have a very special place in the heart of God. Luke 18:15, 16 says, *"People were also bringing babies to Jesus to have him touch them. When the disciples saw this, they rebuked them. But Jesus called the children to him and said, 'Let the little children come to me, and do not hinder them, for the kingdom of God belongs to such as these.'"* And we know His sobering words in Mark 9:42, *"And if anyone causes one of these little ones who believe in me to sin, it would be better for him to be thrown into the sea with a large millstone tied around his neck."*

God loves the little ones in a very special way, yet He trusts us to nurture them into the fullness of the potential that He placed within them. While He does not expect us to be perfect in anything we do, it is a very serious thing for us to hinder them or to handicap them by the way in which we attempt to impart godliness to them.

Each new little one, who arrives in a body which we give a name, comes with a light in his or her soul. The light of life which is connected to God Himself.

This light, if properly cared for and nourished, will become strong and bright. It will be fueled by the Presence of God and expressed in a life of righteousness, peace, and joy—thereby revealing the glory of God everywhere it goes in this dark world.

However, similar to starting a campfire in the wind or rain, we must protect and help this little flame. We might even say that because of our sinful disposition, it's something like building a fire with damp wood. It's a nasty world out there for these flickering little flames! Our task is overwhelming.

Part of the sacred trust in the adult/child relationship is the almost frightening power a child gives us to impart personal worth to them. They allow us to tell them who they are or are not. What they can or cannot become. That he or she is or is not a beautiful person. It is imperative that we take the assignment seriously. Jesus is watching.

Because of the way in which the home, church, and school contribute to the concept that a teen forms about God and the church, we must accurately represent Him to them. He is a God of grace, kindness, mercy, and every other expression of love.

Our greatest responsibility is to fan and fuel the fire that grows through the child's knowledge of and relationship with God, but it is easy for us to get sidetracked and to focus on cultural and institutional rules and expectations. We quickly become rules-driven and even authoritarian.

If the home, church, and school are all such, it is likely that youth will walk away from the church and even from God. In fact, it is a wonder that any of The Few survive. We have allowed the fire to be nearly blown out or to be starved for fuel.

If the home is somewhat grace and mentoring based, there is more hope. And there is room for real optimism if parents help their teens sort things out as suggested here, even if the school or church are authoritarian.

"God Help the Little Ones!"

My brother Karl and I ruminate on these things sometimes. He observes that although we grew up in such a denomination and attended a strict Christian high school, we had some major points of "relief" that helped us stay in the church all these years. To start with, we lived on the outskirts of the conservative community. There wasn't much "pressure" in our everyday life. And Father was a Christian but wasn't much bothered by legalistic rules. Mother didn't grow up in a conservative home, which avoided the baggage that many of our friends' mothers had. She was faithful to the church but was more concerned about being Christian than legalistic.

Another major factor was our pastor. Because of some of the other church leaders over us and the denominational culture in general, I was given the sense of a very stern, almost harsh, and certainly judgmental God. Fortunately, while Pastor Noah Hershey was loyal to the denomination he was also warm and understanding, and because of that he helped me feel better about the church. His influence kept a door open in my mind through which God could speak to me of His incredible and persistent kindness. It is true that Christian parents and school and church leaders communicate a lot to their youth about the nature of God and *His* rules by their own rules and the way in which they are applied.

Unfortunately, too many of Karl's and my high school classmates and others of our generation "got it" at home, in the church, and at school. I grieve at the thought of the alienation it created in some of them—alienation from the joyful and fulfilling life which comes from the bright light of God within—from the richness of personhood that

He had created them to walk in. For many, this means alienation from the church and for some, alienation from Him forever.

Those who perpetuate such a mindset today, in any Christian institution, ought to seriously consider the impact they have upon God's little ones. The hunger of the human soul is for fellowship with God, which is the fuel for the flickering light in the soul of the little one. When we misrepresent that and make it religion instead of relationship, we diminish its beauty and appeal—and sometimes at great cost.

For more please see Afterwords C: "God Help the Grownups!"

part three

For Adults Only

15	Three Fingers Pointing Back
16	The Dark Side of Power
17	God's Way Versus Satan's Way
18	So, Which Is It?

This is certainly the heaviest section in this book and one I would have preferred to do without. But it needs to be said. Please read it thoughtfully and with an open heart, remembering that conviction and condemnation are two very different things.

Conviction is from God and focuses on an inappropriate attitude or action. Its sole purpose is to lead us to new life by identifying something which distances us from godliness, giving us opportunity to repent, and then lifting us to a higher level of life in Christ. Wow—we ought to welcome that!

Condemnation is very different. It focuses on us personally rather than on our action. "You are a bad *person*," instead of "You did a bad thing." It continues, "*You* are a failure" or, "Look at you;

you did it *again*." Condemnation is from Satan and its sole purpose is to stomp us and crush us. It drives us down and distances us from God.

It is likely that you will hear both God and Satan as you read this book, and especially these four chapters. Please listen only to God and let Him speak words of conviction and new life to you. I beg you, don't receive words of condemnation, regardless of the measure in which these chapters may challenge you.

chapter fifteen

Three Fingers Pointing Back

We need to remember that when we point an accusing finger at our restless teens, three fingers are pointing back at us.

Our youth have an appetite for "life". The more life-giving their environment, the more they will need to be truly rebellious in order to want out of it. In what measure have we made walking with God appealing to them? Are we modeling a victorious and joyful Christian life? Are we trying to lead them into an intimate relationship with Jesus—or to our culture, set of beliefs, and standards of conduct?

Teens *must* look outside of our established beliefs, values, and ways of doing things in the process of selecting their own. That's where they get the options that are part of their development. Our role is to influence them through instruction, consistent example, encouragement, and correction—but we must refuse the compulsion to control them. The measure to which they distance themselves from us will be shaped by their personality, their comfort level with the information they already have, and the degree to which we insist on holding them close to us versus giving the freedom they need.

It goes without saying that there are a small number of teens who by this time are hardened and who reject most authority because of emotional, physical, or sexual abuse—sometimes by those in authority over them. Others have suffered the trauma of parents in conflict, divorce, being "lost" in a blended family, the death of a parent or similar experiences. And there are some inherent risks which may come with adoption.* All need and deserve careful understanding and possibly extensive counseling. They weren't formed that way by God, so obviously something negative took place along the way—and most likely at the hand of adults. We sometimes forget that every one of these kids has gold somewhere deep within and write them off when the effect of what they have experienced impacts our institution. They deserve better.

There's another sobering possibility about why kids act the way they do. As a tree is known by its fruit, children are very much the product of their parents and their home environment. They make their own choices, but they don't make them out of thin air.

I fear being judged as laying inappropriate guilt upon parents by saying this, so please try to understand my intent—which is to be an advocate for kids. My sense is that we often look at children and how their actions affect the institution without being realistic about why they are the way they are. I believe that parents must more actively seek to understand, and must accept greater responsibility for how their private lives, family traits, or cultural expectations affect the child.

On the more honorable side, it shouldn't surprise anyone that a teen from an adventurous family would struggle with boundaries. A family culture of handling motorcycles, four-wheelers, boats, or other vehicles in a daring way may well create in the child a need for more excitement than an institution welcomes. Isn't it true that sometimes "rebellious kids" are just bored kids?

Or it may be that a child is expressing a positive family trait, but simply hasn't yet learned how to do it in a healthy and productive way in a social setting. Is the family competitive or fun-loving and maybe even given to pranks? Are they a talkative or expressive family? Do they experiment and seek knowledge?

And who of us wouldn't agree that birth order, including the gender of siblings and age difference, impacts a child?

On the less honorable side, our child might be living out an unhealthy attitude, desire, or fantasy that lies deep within an adult they relate to. Pride; a general disregard for the value of others; or issues of a sexual nature come to mind. An unwed, pregnant daughter, or the guy who got her pregnant, may be living out secret passions in a father or mother. Parents may have been able to suppress it or hide it in a certain way, but it's there and it affects the child because it is spirit in nature. At this point in life teens may be honest or unrestrained enough to do what their parents would really *like* to do, but don't do because of personal conscience, cultural expectations, or institutional consequences. And possibly something that was only a small, underground root in us has borne fruit in them.

Parents' attitude toward speed limits, church rules, or other expressions of authority over them will predictably influence the teen's response to rules and authority. Parents who stretch or compromise the truth can easily produce children who carry this trait to the next level. Those who go to church because they should, or who are frequently critical of the church or its leadership, can't be surprised if their kids don't want to go at all. They have not yet bowed to the power of "should" in the way their parents have.

We as parents also need to accept responsibility if we place our children under church, school, or other authorities who relate to them in an unjust or negative way. We're still the parent and the one most directly accountable to God for their welfare.

Adults need to understand these factors, and while they don't vindicate restless teens or give license for unrestrained freedom, taking them into account can bring understanding and shape how we respond. It will help us nurture them as the individual they are, rather than quickly judging them as rebellious. *"Mercy triumphs over judgment,"* as we read in James 2:13, is a powerful, life-giving principle!

I've heard parents "wash their hands" of responsibility in regard to their child's actions. I would discourage that without first doing some deep, humble soul-searching. "Has anything in me given opportunity for that expression in my child?" Sometimes that becomes very personal.

God has chastened me more than once through the years when I wanted to place a judgment on a son. Years ago I heard one of them speak to the other in a demeaning way. It angered me but I held my peace. As I left their place of business and drove up the road, God said, "Do you know why that made you so mad? It's because he did it just like you do it." I was alone, but I flushed with embarrassment and felt physically hot, as though He had said it to me in front of an audience. I repented of that pattern of speech, prayed for freedom in our family, and have never heard it since.

It is said that the thing we most dislike in others may be our own greatest weakness. It is possible for us to unknowingly exercise control over our children to keep them from being like us. A better and more effective way is to confess our weakness, repent of it, and break its generational power in those who follow us.

I have grown into an "always Dad" theory which says that as long as I draw breath, God's ongoing work in my life will influence those who follow me. I've seen it too often to deny it, convenient as that might be. I actively walk in the awareness that as I find new life in any attitude, habit, or other weakness which marks our family, it is available to those behind me. Every family has such marks and each generation has power to disable them and replace them with something better for subsequent generations. Exodus 34:7b is a truth to be reckoned with. Taken alone it would seem to condemn, but it can also be taken as a warning and can drive us toward verses 6 and 7a, which speak hope for change.

Isn't there something exhilarating about that? If Romans 8:28 is true, a child's "problems" can be viewed as a potential opportunity for us as parents to go deeper in our own walk with God. Our youth's hunger for authenticity can be the needed stimulus for us to break out of some of our paper bags of legalism, superficiality, or unwise cultural or religious expectations. Possibly sin is being shouted from the mountaintop and there is an attitude or action that we need to repent of. We certainly can't impart to them a measure of godliness that we don't have ourselves!

Obviously we can't trace every issue in the life of a child back to a parent or other adult, but it's probably true often enough that it ought to mellow our attitude and soften our judgment as we respond to them.

Certainly the way in which our influence is expressed changes when our children become adults, but there is still great power in our modeling, and in the impact that our action has in the spirit realm! Because of the way in which God designed humanity and the spirit world, authority is available to us in a measure equal to the level of responsibility we are given and which we accept. No more, no less.

We adults have everything to gain for ourselves and our teens by embracing this principle of honesty, repentance, and change as we move together toward greater Christlikeness. Another obvious option is to ignore our own potential culpability in our children's issues and use our leadership power to control them and compel them to move in the "right" direction. We covered "control" some in Chapter 3, "Invisible, Odorless—and Deadly," and we'll probe further into the subject now.

*Please see Afterwords D: "Potential Risks with Adoption."

chapter sixteen

The Dark Side of Power

Sin occurs when something that God created for our good and His glory is distorted or perverted for Satan's purposes.

For example, society needs a medium of exchange, and money is very useful in the extension of God's Kingdom. Jesus used money. But we also know how quickly it can become a master rather than a servant. I Timothy 6:10 even says that, *"The love of money is a root of all kinds of evil."* God receives glory when we choose to make money and possessions servants in our lives, viewing ourselves as stewards rather than owners.

And sex is one of the most spectacular parts of all creation. Its proper use symbolizes the intimacy we were created to enjoy with God in a way that nothing else can, but its perversion brings indescribable pain and brokenness.

The primary purpose of power in relationships is to interface between an individual and the various institutions of society, including the home, school, church, business, nation, and more. Individuals are given authority to empower them to fulfill a responsibility they have been given to educate and train, maintain order, govern, protect, and so forth. When authority is used to serve others in these ways it is beneficial. It builds up the individual and helps him open and flourish like a flower in good soil, moisture, and light.

However, as in the case of money and sex, power can be perverted. It can be used to dominate others for selfish gain. With it we rule and diminish their "person" rather than serving them and building them up. The leadership style that we embrace helps shape the degree to which we will lead by influence or by control.

In some Christian circles there is a strong emphasis on the authority of leaders "over" others. Parent to child, husband to wife, pastor to parishioner, teacher or administrator to student, and so on. That is appropriate in a certain way depending on several factors, but in my judgment it is frequently over emphasized.

There are many ways to say many things, but please consider this attempt to diagram the flow of authority and relationships. While it is certainly incomplete in expressing every facet of leadership authority, it might help you evaluate and diagram your own approach.

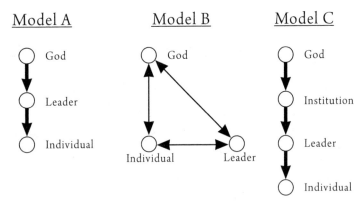

Model A portrays an authority-driven, downward flow from God to the leader, to the individual, i.e. a church member, wife, child, student, or other. The leader represents God to the individual and speaks to them on His behalf.

This model is vulnerable to control and authoritarianism as its basic manner of expression because authority comes from position. Hopefully it will be shaped and modified by the spirit of Model B, but that is not always the case. Many Christian institutions, including families, operate on the tenets of Model A. Possibly those who function as a "spiritual head" ought to more actively see their role as being in the spiritual realm, i.e. protecting those under them from spiritual attack and ministering life to them—and less as an everyday ruler over them.

In B, we have the leader to the side, serving the individual in his or her walk with God. I intentionally put double-headed arrows on B, but not A, to indicate a very different kind of flow. Here, a leader views himself as serving others in their walk with God, as he himself walks with God. This is a relationship-driven model as compared to the position-driven approach in A. It is quite "warm" in comparison to A and seems much closer to the "influence" approach that God uses with us, which we'll discuss shortly. Authority comes primarily from relationship. Close your eyes, "soak" on these two diagrams, and feel the profound difference!

Parenting is a mixture of A and B. We work in Model A with younger children, using B as much as possible. As they grow we must shift toward B, and certainly that must be the primary model as they advance into their teen years, with our only dropping back to A in a few instances.

Consider this too. Model B connects the individual directly to God in terms of the enabling power of His presence in their life, and the sense of accountability to

Him. When they fail, He responds to them with mercy, understanding, and love-based discipline. Model A is more likely to connect the individual to the leader and/or the institution for both power to do well and for accountability. However, they have far less power to help and are often more rules and fear-driven than love-driven.

As a pastor, I would draw this out in my first counseling session with someone. While I wanted to hear and speak the heart of God to them, and it seemed that He gave me insights that I would have no other way of knowing, it was all for the sole purpose of nurturing their walk with Him and helping them come free from hindrances. I wanted them to become most dependent upon and accountable to Him, not me!

Model B types of institutional leaders (home, church, school) will take this approach as they fulfill their everyday responsibility to nurture, educate, and so forth, but they will shift toward our Model C when disciplinary action is taken toward an individual for their own welfare or that of the many. Authority has now shifted somewhat from relational to positional. While I show downward pointing arrows only, indicating the flow of authority, it would hopefully be expressed in a relational spirit, which would need double-headed arrows.

Okay, here's a big one. Whose rules are they? Parents and church and school leaders frequently write rules as though they are the rules of God and enforce them as though they themselves are the voice of God—when they are truthfully only the rules of the institution. This is very serious. We need institutional rules and we must enforce them for the welfare of the individual and the group, but it is desperately important that we don't give them a spiritual weight that they don't deserve. When we try to play God in the life of another we become authoritarian and controlling, because that's how we get the power to subjugate them to our will.

As Satan rose up against God, the controlling individual rises up against the image of God in another human being. It is incredibly easy for parents and others to use authority or position-driven control instead of relationally based influence when fulfilling their responsibility toward a child. And certainly control joins judgmentalism at the top of the list of the most destructive things that Christians do to each another.

This isn't a nice thing to say, but my hypothesis is that "influence" is God's way of getting us to where He wants us, and "control" is Satan's way of getting us to where *he* wants us. Let's take a look at that.

chapter seventeen

God's Way Versus Satan's Way

Everything God asks us to do is for our good, including the "Thou shalt nots." And think about how patiently and gently He speaks to us and urges us on. He is the God of Psalm 145:8-21, Jeremiah 9:24, Exodus 34:6, 7, and Psalm 36:5-7 and 51:1. If you haven't thought of Him in that way it's probably because of a false concept imparted to you by a controlling authority in your life.

Everything God speaks to us is 100% truth. He is total wisdom and He knows everything about everything, yet He does not force Himself upon us. He invites us to choose the good life by following His voice and walking in His ways. He wants us to be informed and to consider the consequences of our actions, but He gives us the freedom to make our own choices and to experience their results. That's what "influence" is, and it represents a blend of genuine concern for another and respect for their personhood and free will.

Satan disregards our individual personhood and general welfare. He is the epitome of what it means to be self-centered. He wants unthinking obedience and tries to force himself upon us. He lies to us about the consequences of doing his will.

What are the areas where *you* have felt his attempts at control? Think about the buffet, boutique, beach, or bookrack and the way in which his will is almost forced upon your actions. *That* is what control is! It is the attempt to usurp the free will of another. And *that* describes what takes place when those with power control those under them. Scary, isn't it?

If you are in conflict with one who is under your power and/or authority, please sit quietly somewhere and consider the contrast between influence and control as presented above. Relive some exchanges you've had and judge your responses by these principles.

One does not need to be among history's ruthless and almost demonic dictators in order to exercise control. It is possible for sincere Christians to unknowingly slide into this mode in order to help teens or others under their authority to act in a desirable manner. By doing so we usurp the place of God in their lives.

Control is one means of achieving goals—even honorable ones. Many religious groups practice it as part of keeping members and/or their children in the group. Fear is a common dominator in such a culture, i.e. the fear of personal rejection, the loss of various forms of security, and more.

Sometimes control is expressed for its own sake alone; that is, as part of expressing personal superiority, but in most cases there is reward or supposed reward of some kind. In all cases such control diminishes individuals and keeps them from being the person they could otherwise be. Control masquerading as concern is still control, and it can be hidden behind a humble front or expressed in a pseudo-spiritual manner.

Adults may truly believe that their rules, boundaries, and expectations are for the welfare of the child, and they probably are in a significant way. However, any self-interest, or lack of respect for the "person" of the teen, can shift them from influence toward control in the way they exercise leadership. It immediately becomes counter-productive in the development of the child. This is an extremely delicate issue requiring regular and honest evaluation of our methods—and humble trust in God's way, which is influence. If it feels like we have given up personal control, it's because we have—but in doing so we've become more like God Himself!

Control is a way of handling relationships. Of posturing oneself in relation to others. Because of how it meets an inner need of the one controlling, it can be an addiction of sorts. Those who recognize the tendency to express control will do well to be alert to ways in which it can pop up even after confessed and dealt with in a specific situation.

"Control" as used here is never a good thing. It is very different from setting reasonable rules and expectations and enforcing them justly, even to the extent of corporal punishment. (Yes, I embrace the "spare the rod, spoil the child" principle of Proverbs.) It has to do with the spirit in which authority is expressed and the motive behind it.

As discussed in "The Mandate," our role as adults is to train up a child in the way he or she should go, and that certainly includes our expression of authority. However, a parent who struggles with the issues raised in that chapter can easily succumb to control in an effort to move their teen in the direction they are more comfortable with.

"What others think" is a dominating motivation for

many parents. Their need for approval by others in order to feel good about themselves, or successful as a parent, can quickly shape their response to a child's actions.

And think about this. We would agree, wouldn't we, that beautiful women and handsome men are more vulnerable to the temptation to pride than we more ordinary folks? That goes with the territory. Likewise, parents, institutional leaders and others who are highly motivated or gifted, or who do things really well, or who have strong ambitions of some kind for their children can easily slip into control as a means of helping them advance according to plan. It goes with the territory.

They and other authorities will benefit by actively and honestly searching their hearts along the way to determine if influence or control is being used when nurturing those they are responsible for. Because of its subtle and deep-reaching nature, identifying and repenting of this tendency is among the most difficult challenges that many Christians will face in their whole lifetime.

Would you agree that control is a factor in many kids becoming truly rebellious, running away, or taking their own life? They are not allowed to be the person they were created to be, and which they must become in order to be whole. They are forced to live with an unbearable tension between the person they truly are and the person others compel them to try to be. Rebelling, running away or taking their own life seems to be the only way out—and in reality, depending on personalities and the specific situation, that might almost be true. They don't want to die, nor are they able to continue to live that way.

chapter eighteen

So, Which Is It?

A good way to tell whether we are practicing influence or control is by how we respond when our attempt at leadership is challenged or refused.

Compassion and sorrow are expressions of selfless concern for another's welfare. We are grieved because of the confusion and pain they are experiencing, rather than angry because of the impact of their actions upon us. We fear for them because we know the likely consequences that lie ahead if they continue on this path, rather than fearing what others think of us because of their action. We are sad because we know that by their choices they are missing, and could continue to miss, the abundant life that comes from walking God's path. Our anger is toward spiritual forces which have moved the child toward this conduct. We may lie awake some at night, but our thoughts and concerns will be love-driven, not self-centered. Our tears are those of compassion, not self-pity. We are disappointed *for* them more than *in* them. And as we pray and encourage, we will humbly search our hearts for ways in which we may have contributed to their attitudes or actions.

If we are moving from influence, our response to a child's misconduct might be to create further opportunities for influence. Our natural tendency is to pull back when we experience tension with a child, but a better option is to deliberately create some bridges between ourselves and them. Some points where we can connect even if we are distanced in certain ways: Spending time together and imparting skills by working on mechanical, woodworking, or other projects, or cutting firewood together for a young man to sell create incredible opportunitie to communicate acceptance and impart worth to him.

Elaine and I have three sons but there are comparable things that one would do with a daughter. Preparing meals that the child particularly enjoys, going places they are interested in, playing games they like and similar activities are effective—and all without making a point of why we're doing it.

There are many ways to strengthen our influence, but a common denominator is that we'll need to give the child a higher level of priority in our life—and that alone will speak volumes. We have approached them from the standpoint that *their* need is *our* need and we thus accept some responsibility for their struggles. They will know that without our saying it. The more we do these kinds of things the less we'll need to talk about the issues, because by these actions we will reinforce words and values we have previously communicated.

On the other hand, a parent or other's anger toward one who has violated their expectations is more likely an indicator of control than of pure concern for the child. Relational separation; sharp, hostile, demeaning, or condemning words; angry threats; and words or even thoughts like, "How could you do that to me?" are dead giveaways. Beware when your stomach begins to churn and your eyes begin to narrow! And don't give your anger any other name! These are symptoms of control, just as nausea and dizziness warn us of carbon monoxide poisoning.

If it is anger at teens, it's very likely because we can't control them and they're getting to us. It is their will versus ours, and our anger is rising up to defend our position, authority, and ego. Parents and others in authority lower themselves and diminish their effectiveness when they engage in a power struggle with a child. We step out of our God-given position of responsibility and authority and become more of a peer with our fellow combatant. We might win the battle in a certain way because we have positional power, but we will lose the war. In life in general, if we refuse to lower ourselves to the level of combat that someone invites us to, we might lose the immediate battle, but we'll win in the end. I understand that, and not from reading about it in a book! Read Psalm 37:1-11.

Parents who control pay a price too. In my experience with my sons in the early years of our/their business, I had deep physical pain in my gut and many sleepless hours in bed until God showed me the source of our conflict and I dealt with it.

It is widely accepted that stress and frustration have physical, emotional, and spiritual consequences. Restless nights take their toll. Parents suffer in various ways when they are unable to control their child, and it ought to be taken as a warning sign. I know of a father who desperately wanted his adult son to be in business with him. The son was called to ministry abroad, and unknown to him, the father told a mutual friend that if he accepted the call, it would kill him (the father). The son said "Yes," and the father died two weeks later of heart failure.

We can learn a lot about ourselves by listening to our words and feeling our emotions when observing, correcting, or even discussing another. The administrator who had a problem with Charles turned beet red with anger when someone told him that most people experienced Charles as a kind and respectful young man.

Challenging? Yes, incredibly so, but that's the adult task! We have power in relation to children and it's for one purpose—that we would "Train up a child in the way he should go, and in keeping with his individual gift or bent." Dealing with our own weaknesses and faults as we attempt to fulfill that mandate creates some of our own greatest opportunities to be more fully transformed into the image of Christ.

part four

Helping Restless Teens Understand Themselves

	They Need to Know That:
19	We Value Them for the Person They Are
20	They Have Predictable Vulnerabilities
21	They Will Have Some Social Challenges
22	There Are Keys to Their Success

It is important that we *all* understand our individual personality and how it impacts life and relationships, but because they are so often misunderstood and at odds with others, it is especially true for The Few.

Teens could not verbalize what I am telling you about them—nor could I have at their age, but fifty plus years of trying to sort oneself out, and observing countless others, does help. The next four chapters cover some keys to understanding and mentoring those youth who look outside of our boundaries. If we embrace the principles in this book we can save them many years of personal frustration and of being handicapped in their service to our Lord Jesus. These are general statements which will apply to specific individuals in varying degrees and in different ways as the years go by.

As you work through these, please consider that each of us has potential strengths and areas where we lack strength, based on personality, gifts, training, life experiences, and more. In a fairly predictable way, each area of personal strength is accompanied by an area where we will lack strength. For example, is there a principle in the joke, "Did you hear about the absentminded professor who poured molasses down his back and scratched his pancakes?" Isn't there often a dimension of absentmindedness about those who have the focus and intellect of professors, at least in certain areas of academia?

One of my life sayings is, "The lack of strength in a certain area is not an actual weakness unless we deny it and refuse to allow persons with complementary gifts to come alongside us. Otherwise it is simply a characteristic of the individual as he or she is part of the whole." Please bear that in mind as we proceed.

For observations on "The Few as Adults" please see Afterwords E with that title.

chapter nineteen

We Value Them for the Person They Are

Because each person is formed by the hand of God to express His image in a uniquely special way, these principles apply to teens in general and they need to be emphasized during the years when they are becoming more independent in their choices.

Parents begin the most important role in life with little or no training or experience, and some are blessed with a child who is challenged by rules and boundaries more than others! If these children are not properly understood and nurtured they can easily spend their whole life at a lower level than God intended. All children from the cradle up, but especially The Few, need to know that:

• They are fearfully and wonderfully made, and the basic drive within them is good. God put it there. That drive is needed in society and in the Kingdom of God and we value it highly. Please, please, please—they need to hear that from us often, in attitude and word.

• We will respect, affirm, and bless that inner person even if it doesn't always come out just right. We will give our children freedom to grow in understanding and expressing the unique person they are, and will practice an accepting and forgiving heart toward them as God does toward us. However, they need to help us by being teachable.

- We will nurture them into the distinct person that God intends them to be, even if that is different from us or from what we might have dreamed of for them. It is okay for them to be different from us.
- We are willing to do some growing and adjusting ourselves as we help them learn to experience and express their individual personhood. They will need to be patient with us as we try to figure them out, and as we process our own responses to them.
- We will acknowledge when we fail and misjudge them and attempt to make them into someone with whom we are personally more comfortable.

Probably the best way for some parents and other authorities to initiate such a relationship with a teen is to ask forgiveness for their past failures on these points.

chapter twenty

They Have Predictable Vulnerabilities

You already know how much I value The Few and their ability to contribute to us. However, a principle of life would say that their great potential for good implies an accompanying potential for difficulty. We need to be serious about their inherent risks. They need to know that:

• Their gift makes them vulnerable to breaking rules which really do need to be kept. Disregarding rules can be a way by which they define themselves, even if it means to mark themselves as troublesome. If they are not wise they can slide into lawlessness more easily than others. We *all* need boundaries and authority for our safety and personal well-being, and to maintain order in society. They must refuse the mindset that they can write their own rules or be a law unto themselves. While we affirm their outward-looking spirit and always seeking a "better way," we caution them against recklessness and irresponsible disregard for rules. That is neither wise nor godly, but it is a temptation they will face more than others.

• They will be tempted to ignore consequences of their actions. Often there are physical, financial, and relational costs when we don't give proper respect to conventional rules and boundaries, many of which are part of God's creation design. He laid down physical laws such as the law of gravity, relational laws such as respecting others, the principle of sowing and reaping, and many more. Every human thought, word, or deed bears its own fruit and they must be realistic about that. We must find creative and positive ways to help them learn the reality of consequences.

- Because of the way in which they look "out there" for something new and exciting, they may, more than others, find it hard to follow through on commitments. They may also overlook details in a way that frustrates others. Both of these are important and will require conscious attention and openness to more detail-oriented persons who can be a respecting and complimentary partner or mentor in their lives. Often a spouse can partner with them.
- They will be tempted toward individualism. While we bless them as individuals, they must guard against individualism, i.e. the attitude, "I will be me regardless of what others think or how it affects them."
- They will be tempted to try to vindicate themselves through logic and argument when they are misunderstood and accused. That's a big topic, but the harder they try the worse it will get. Their greatest hope is to "walk godly" and let Him vindicate them over time. They can choose to be a "Psalm 37 man", or woman. Read it – it works.
- We all have a need for approval, but it can take on an unhealthy dimension. The Few must find their deepest sense of identity and well-being in their relationship with God and in being the person He wants them to be. He has created them with this outward-looking approach to life, and He has a purpose for them. *People* may be uncomfortable with them but He is not. Friends may

turn away from them, but He will not. While they must constantly learn to relate to others in a better way, they will often need to choose to allow the negative responses of people to drive them toward God. *He* is their pool in the desert, their shelter in the storm, their vitality and confidence when people reject or attack them. Any other choice will lead to disaster.

If they are not able to find their identity in who they are before God and are driven by the need for approval from people, they will find themselves acting unwisely in various ways to try to win that approval. For example, they might offer suggestions in a setting where such are simply not welcomed, and create even greater distance between themselves and others. Or they can lower themselves and become a conformist. That doesn't work either. It will backfire on them because they are trying to be someone they are not.

chapter twenty-one

They Will Have Some Social Challenges

One of the goals of Christian adults is to help our children develop social skills for the Kingdom of God. Our more aggressive and outward-looking youth present us with some particular challenges in this regard, and we need to act wisely. Here are some points that I believe will help us in mentoring them. They need to know that:

• They are different from many others, which will affect relationships including fellow students, teachers, and youth leaders, as well as their co-workers and employers in the workplace. People may misunderstand their apparent confidence and interpret them as being aloof or independent, not realizing that they desperately want to be in relationship—yet accepted as the core person they are. This risk must be accepted realistically and The Few need to give people time to learn to know them.

• They will make some folks uncomfortable with their questions and suggestions, especially the more naturally compliant institutional leadership found in social-based institutions such as churches, schools, and sometimes the workplace. That's just the way it is, but they can reduce that risk by understanding others better than they are understood themselves, and by being prudent in how and when they speak.

- Although The Few might not *feel* respect for an individual because of closed-mindedness, the rigid application of seemingly irrelevant rules, or patterns of inconsistency, injustice, or hypocrisy, they still need to respect the person's years, virtues, position, and service. Expressing outright disrespect is unacceptable.

chapter twenty-two

There Are Keys to Their Success

The Few are responsible to act wisely as they live, work, and minister among others. Developing the following attitudes and skills will be a lifelong pilgrimage for most, but the journey will be so much better for all as they learn to:

• Value the ideas of others. They need to practice meekness with their boldness if they expect to influence others. They can empower their idea by flowing it into the insights of others or diminish its potential by discounting others' views.

• Avoid pushing an idea that is not actually a good idea. It is true that no idea is a bad idea unless it turns out not to be a good idea, and you still insist on it—but it's also true that they will have some ideas that turn out not to be good ideas!

• Work as part of a team. While they may be full of countless "better ideas," they will be much more successful if they learn to work in concert with others. They are only part of the whole. They need those who are more attuned to how their idea will impact existing organizational structures and ways of doing things. I have never done anything "big time" in my life, but any worthwhile accomplishments were possible only because of those with complementary gifts whom God allowed me to team up with. While I was at times the "idea guy" in a certain way, these business, ministry, and educational efforts would not have succeeded without the insight and effort of others. Most successful leaders, even company founders and CEOs, are team players and depend on the gifts of others. A free-thinking aircraft engineer can design a wonderful new airplane, but he will fail if he doesn't team up with management and marketing people.

- Measure risk and potential gain and choose their battles carefully. A loose cannon on deck is a danger to all. There is often more than one good way to do things and not everything needs to be done in a new way! Some ideas are simply not worth fighting for in terms of effort, potential gain, and risk.
- Feel and express *righteous* anger toward what seems to be ongoing injustice, hypocrisy, and abuse of power. Anger is a God-given emotion to help empower us to defend and protect. There is both righteous and unrighteous anger. Righteous anger is expressed when we defend/protect truth, godliness, innocence, justice and so forth. Unrighteous anger is when we defend/protect selfish pride and ego. Righteous anger can degenerate into unrighteous anger and bitterness, and it can be expressed in an unrighteous way. The Few *will* experience anger at times when others don't, and they ought to cherish that ability. They also need to regularly search their hearts to be sure it is *righteous* anger, and even then to discern in what form it is best expressed. For example, it might be intercessory prayer, a word of encouragement to the one who is being offended, confronting the offenders, or going to those in authority over them.

part five

Wrapping It Up

23   The Battle Is the Lord's
24   The Flight Instructor

       Conclusion

chapter twenty-three

The Battle Is the Lord's

Everyone wants to know God, and God wants everyone to know Him. If our children have any knowledge of Him at all, and if we have nurtured them and are praying for them, we must believe that He is actively at work in their lives. And we must believe that, although it may not appear to be so, they desperately want to be in relationship with Him. Every human was created with that hunger.

We must choose to stay out of the way enough to give God room to work. We must trust His Holy Spirit to work in them, often affirming and calling them to the things that we are teaching them and modeling for them. It feels risky. Terribly risky. But no one knows them as He does, or loves them more, or is better able to call them to righteousness. That is a rock of truth that we must choose to stand on, and our choice will profoundly influence the child's ability to move toward Him.

I have, at several crossroads in my life, been instructed, corrected, and empowered by the truths of Psalm 37, especially vv 1-11. However, I maintain that Christians often find it easier to believe in the power of evil than righteousness. We see our teens surrounded by Satan's influences of immorality, dishonesty, greed, and other expressions of broken humanity. We fear for them and take things into our own hands. And we ought to fear—but in a different way.

We need to fear the Lord even more than we fear the evil

Wrapping It Up

around our youth! As Solomon said in Proverbs 1:7: *"The fear of the Lord is the beginning of knowledge, but fools despise wisdom and instruction."* That is, we are to respect the laws and principles that God initiated when He formed the earth and created man, and fear the consequences of ignoring them. Throughout this book I have attempted to communicate what I believe to be some of the mind of God in relation to children becoming adults, and the role and responsibility of adults who nurture them through that process.

If we fear God, we will believe and act upon several key principles. If we act upon these principles, He will aggressively work in the minds and hearts of our youth and help them choose His ways. Here are three key points of belief and action. We should not blame the kids for the results of our failure in these areas.

1) Parents and other adult authorities in the life of a teen must pray often, including serious spiritual intercession. In Ephesians 6:12 Paul writes: *"For our struggle is not against flesh and blood, but against the rulers, against the powers, against the world forces of this darkness, against the spiritual forces of wickedness in the heavenly places."* It is truly a spiritual battle. Prayer and spiritual warfare are for real. They do change things. We err when we try to substitute rules and control for what we ought to be achieving through prayer. If Christian institutions took this seriously, our boards would probably shift some emphasis from "major donors" to "committed spiritual intercessors."

2) We adults must walk in godliness and integrity ourselves. "Tell" has not replaced "show and tell" in the nurturing process. "Follow me as I follow Christ" is a

Biblical principle, but "Do as I say, not as I do" is not. The measure in which we allow hypocrisy in our own lives will directly diminish the effectiveness of our teaching, our enforcement of rules, and other efforts to equip teens to walk well with God. They will find it hard to respect the authority of adults whose lives demonstrate inconsistencies in any one of many ways. There is no substitute for our own humble and sincere pursuit of Him in an active spiritual pilgrimage—even as we nurture them:

- Refusing to use the power of position to cover our own egos, weaknesses, or immaturity;
- Determining to use influence rather than control; and
- Humbly acknowledging when we are wrong.

3) We must believe that wisdom, truth, and righteousness have their own voice, empowered by God Himself. We must trust that these voices, as heard through our teaching, example, and godly discipline, and through the Scriptures, music, and other media, will, if backed up by 1 and 2 above, impact our teens at least as effectively as the evil around them. Do we believe that? If not, read Psalm 37:1-11 again. And again. "Bad" doesn't have the last word for those who trust God. "Good" does—if we will give it room and time to work. God *wants* to fight our battles for us with these weapons (wisdom, truth, and righteousness). He longs to get between us and the enemy, as He did for Israel on so many occasions, but we don't let Him do it. As Israel, we too often fight the battle ourselves—and with the same terrible but predictable results.

If you are interested in doing some Bible study on the topic of the heart and hand of God on behalf of His own, please see: Afterwords F: The Heart and Hand of God.

chapter twenty-four
The Flight Instructor

I've done flight instructing from time to time since 1963 and there are some interesting parallels between that and nurturing teens. Each section below embodies a principle that can be applied to parents and other authorities who relate to our youth. Let your mind drift back and forth between these illustrations and the teens you walk with and see if you can find the applications.

I treasure my copy of the 1956 *Flight Instructor's Handbook,* C.A.A. Technical Manual No. 105. It begins with this introduction: "Teaching is one of the oldest arts. Only recently, however, has man attempted to develop the art of instruction into a system of efficient procedures and processes which will produce predictable results. Principles of education have been developed which apply equally to all teaching, whether it be that of singing a song or flying a transport airplane." Could we replace "singing a song" with "raising children?"

And then here's the first paragraph in the main text: "The flight instructor's first step in teaching is to gain the confidence of his student. If he fails to gain the confidence and respect of a student, any instruction he gives him will be ineffective." Wow! Does this principle apply to adults in the life of a child?

In flight training we approach every new student with the mindset that we are preparing them to fly by themselves; we are giving them a foundation that will enable them to advance into more complex aircraft; and they must have a safe flying career. Anything less is contrary to the very spirit of what flight training is about. This mentality affects every aspect of the process and it is a responsibility that we accept as a flight instructor.

Flight training is something we do deliberately, and with a plan. We actively impart knowledge and help them develop skills, much like the "train up a child" of Proverbs 22:6. We have conscious and defined goals and standards. We teach, demonstrate, have the student practice, and then we evaluate. And then we do it again. The focus is always on their advancement and welfare.

The moment of "solo" finally arrives, and often sooner than the student expected. They have shown us that they understand the basics and have the needed skill to fly safely "around the patch." We have the student pull the aircraft off to the side of the runway and announce that it's time for them to do it alone. Both feel some risk. Usually we have them go around three times, and then we go back to the hangar and cut off their shirttail and write their name, solo date, and other info on it as a keepsake. It's a moment to celebrate, and more achievements will follow and will be recognized in various ways.

Bear in mind that we didn't yet let them get a friend and fly somewhere for lunch. They were only to take off, fly the traffic pattern, and land, three times—all in the instructor's view. As their skills develop, they will gain additional freedom and responsibility. I well remember the first time I sat back in the cabin of the Cessna 402B (twin engine) with the rest of the family, with two sons in the cockpit. It was one of numerous lines we crossed as my sons' skills advanced, and it was something that I did deliberately.

Most of my flying experience* is in what we call a "taildragger," that is, an aircraft with a tailwheel instead of a nose wheel. The difference between the two is about the same as that between a spirited stallion and an old mare. Or a bicycle versus a tricycle. Actually, an aircraft with a nose wheel is known as having "tricycle gear." Nowadays a pilot needs special training and certification to fly tailwheel aircraft.

While both require skill, a taildragger is less directionally stable on takeoff and landing. It wants to go everywhere but straight down the runway and is a much greater challenge to fly, especially in a crosswind. Some teens, i.e. the more naturally compliant ones, are like a tricycle gear aircraft. They require attention and diligence but not to the degree of our more restless youth. And there are certain vulnerabilities with tricycle gear that you don't have with a tailwheel. Other teens are very much like the taildragger. It is important that we understand the dynamics of the specific aircraft we are dealing with.

Part of the training process is that we need to allow a flight student to develop their skills by learning from their own mistakes. I had an instructor once who fussed at me for every little deviation from his standard, and didn't give me enough "room" to get the feel of it myself. There can be a fine line there, and obviously we don't let them prang the airplane, but learning from our mistakes is an important part of the process. In fact, I wouldn't solo a student until they had gotten at least one good bouncer on landing, giving me the opportunity to teach them how to recover from a bounce!

I did some instructing in a Cessna 180, which fits the "*very* spirited stallion" category. One trainee didn't take me seriously about the need to keep it going straight on the runway. You see, if you let it start to turn, it builds momentum real fast and around you go. Many 180s have been ground-looped, that is, they veered and then spun on around sharply because the pilot didn't maintain directional control. Usually such a maneuver is followed by unpleasant and expensive grinding and crunching sounds.

It became clear that the only way this guy was going to "get the picture," was to let him progress far enough into a ground-loop that he recognized what was happening— and then take the controls myself and straighten it out. It's a bit risky, but it was the only way he would get it. It scared him badly enough that he avoided repeating such an event and went on to become a respectable pilot.

Typically an instructor wants to have his hands and feet off the controls so the student can feel the airplane— but close enough that he can get to them if (when) needed. I started our sons, Ken, Brian, and Mark, in taildraggers. Two soloed in the Piper J-3 Cub and the other in a Super Cub. In the Cub the instructor sits in the front with the student behind him. There are two structural braces just ahead of the front seat, near the instrument panel. One of my techniques was to put my hands up on those braces so the student knew that he "had it." I could get back to the control stick pretty fast, but it communicated the sense that I was depending on him to fly the airplane, and was a confidence builder for him. In other aircraft I try to posture myself in a "relaxed but available" way which expresses the same principle.

The flight instructor relishes situations which challenge his student, because they give opportunity to advance their skills. In the early 1980s we had a little airstrip in a field near Kidron, OH. It was 1300' long, had wires on one end, and some humps. We based a Piper Cub, Super Cub, and Cessna 180 there. At the time, Mark was a Student Pilot, Brian a Private Pilot, and Ken a Commercial Pilot, and all flew out of "Stoltzfus International."

Someone suggested that we could level off the humps, one of which was at an especially bothersome place. It was right at the spot where the aircraft might, or might not, be ready to lift off, depending on load, wind, and other factors. You had to decide each time whether to let the hump "launch" you, so to speak, or to hold the airplane on the ground over the hump, and then lift off beyond it. I said, "No way, that hump teaches you too much about flying." It stayed.

A flight student learns a lot from his instructor, both directly and indirectly. Attitudes, like a commitment to excellence, concern for flight safety, respect for regulations, and regard for other pilots. And habits, like not dragging your brakes while taxiing, straightening up your tailwheel (or nose wheel) when doing your "run up," looking for other aircraft, instrument checks, and much more.

I gained a lot from my father, the late Chris D. Stoltzfus of Coatesville, PA—some taught, some "caught." Father said, "Know what you want the airplane to do, know how to make it do that, and then do it." He modeled a very deliberate approach to flying and expected Karl and me to learn how to handle strong crosswinds and other adverse conditions in a thoughtful way. Father rejected the popular saying: "There are old pilots, and there are bold pilots, but there are no old, bold pilots." We were to understand the risk factors, know how to deal with them, know our limits, and then be bold but careful. In a way that shaped life attitudes for us, he trusted us with advanced aircraft more than many would have.

I did the same with our three sons. Occasionally a friend reminds me of the day when one of our sons, a student pilot at the time, was out practicing takeoffs and landings in the J-3 Cub at the local public airport. It was quite windy, and other more experienced pilots were watching from the office, rather amazed. You only learn to fly in the wind by flying in the wind.

Ken, Brian, and Mark have all been diligent to advance themselves in aviation and to hone their skills far beyond what I could impart to them. I'll admit to having taken deep satisfaction over the years in watching them do things with airplanes—thoughtfully, deliberately and safely—that many others wouldn't do.

Certainly there are significant differences between teaching someone to fly and preparing teens for life, but the parallels are obvious and numerous, aren't they? What difference would it make among teens in the Christian community if we approached them with something of the mindset of a flight instructor as we prepare them for their own solo flight into life?

*For those to whom it means something, most of my 4000 hours are in the Piper J-3 Cub; PA-12 Super Cruiser; PA-18 Super Cub; Cessna 170 and 180; 450-Stearman; T-6G; Twin Beech; Douglas DC-3—with a smattering of Cessna 310, 337 and 402; Thrush; Piper Comanche; Schweizer 2-22 glider; and a few others along the way.

Conclusion

We're talking about serious issues here. Too often we take the easy road by using power to try to subdue restless teens when they make us uncomfortable. We not only miss opportunities to nurture God-given potential, but we actually crush some of them and drive them away from Him.

It is hard for a rules-driven Christian institution to avoid portraying a law-based relationship with God. Said differently, if we have a grace-based relationship with God ourselves, we will be more inclined to use influence in nurturing our children—much to their benefit!

God gave us innocent children. They were created with a yearning to know Him, and to be in fellowship with Him in a way that He becomes their definition of "life" itself. He is to be all of that, in the midst of the nitty-gritty of everyday life. The challenges that we now have with them are the result of the normal development process in conjunction with their life experience, often at the hands of adults. We can be encouraged in knowing that the strength of their resistance toward our rules and boundaries can indicate the strength of their personhood—a force which will enrich all if we nurture it into wholeness.

Most of us know that our kids need hugs. We wrap our arms around them and embrace them. But it needs to be more than physical. We need to wrap our arms around the unique little person that God put in there. The "one and only 'you.'"

Conclusion

The more we affirm, bless, and mentor our teens in the home, school, and church, the better they will understand themselves and accept our nurturing. They will learn to express their individuality in a more healthy way. And the less they will need to push the edges in order to prove that they are who they are. Isn't that a win-win thing?

When conflicts arise and adults unwisely engage the young person in a contest, and it's time for someone to say, "I'm sorry," it just might be that the adult should go first in a humble and sincere spirit, regardless of whether the young person will reciprocate. And please refuse the temptation to use a trivial apology to manipulate the teen into a sincere confession. We've had a lot longer to grow up than they have, and look at us—still wrestling with these kinds of issues!

Discipline is a vital component of the training/mentoring process, but it must be life-giving in both design and application. Nothing I have said is meant to eliminate the need for serious discipline, including in-school detention, or even the expulsion of our teens who persistently and willfully fail to respect rules and authority, and especially when they do that in a way which interferes with the welfare of others. However, I say confidently that the need for such action will be greatly reduced when both our restless teens and those in authority understand and embrace the core message of this book. And obviously adults need to take the first step.

Everybody benefits if we approach discipline in the spirit of nurture rather than punishment alone. Discipline performed in a nurturing spirit is positive, patient, kind, and forward looking. Punishment can also be quite vindictive, reflecting a power struggle between the two individuals in which case it is often done hurriedly and in anger. It is also more backward-looking. A nurturing spirit, even when exercising discipline, will more naturally preserve relationships or at least allow for their restoration, while punishment alone will contribute to relational separation.

We should remember that certain kinds of sexual or other indiscretions are predictable as kids, especially boys, mature physically and discover those of the opposite sex. They need nurturing, i.e. understanding, teaching, and correction, instead of the judgment and angry punishment which are sometimes much easier for us. It is unfortunate when our developing youth need to pay a price for our own discomfort in approaching the topic of sexuality in an open and helpful way.

Overall, we will see very different responses, too, if we practice mercy rather than judgment. James 2:13 says that *"mercy triumphs over judgment,"* but judgment is so much easier because we simply make ourselves the standard and call others to it. (Read the whole verse!)

Mercy is that quality of the heart which enables us to see through the frustrating attitudes and actions of the teen and glimpse the richness that is hidden behind them. If we extend to these teens just a fraction of the mercy that we depend on from God, 24/7/365, it will change the whole dynamic of our relationship with them! Consider the forbearing love of God which covers many of our offenses, giving us time to grow instead of quickly calling us to account for every little misdeed. Think how it would be if He treated us like we treat our youth in this regard!

Conclusion

Certainly every one of us would have long ago been reduced to a little pile of ashes by the heat of His anger toward unrighteousness if it were not for His mercy.

We need a good dose of humility, too, as we walk with these kids. Because of our personal ambitions for them or other preconceived notions about them, we can miss the real person whom God has placed inside their body. And our personal weaknesses or immaturity can influence how we "read" and respond to them. Humility on the part of an adult goes a long ways in our relationship with teens!

And let's remember the power of words to speak blessing or a curse upon a child's inner person. Even a dog responds to tone of voice and countenance and might run away from us with its tail between its legs. Kids too!

Here are some questions to ask ourselves when we're trying to understand a specific conflict situation.

1) Do we truly want our youth to develop their own values for life, and to form their own identity, or *do* we, deep down inside, want them to be just like us?

2) In what measure have we or others tried to control rather than influence them as they move through this stage of life? Have we forced them to resist us as they express a deep, inner, God-driven drive toward forming their own identity?

3) How humble are we willing to be, and how hard are we willing to work to create an environment in which they can grow in a positive way—without having to learn so much from their own mistakes?

4) Acknowledging our tendency to misjudge them, what *is* truly going on in the mind, heart, and emotions of the teen with whom we are in conflict?

5) What is it about a certain rule or boundary that makes it easier or more difficult to obey?

6) What is it about a certain authority figure that inclines a teen to want to please, or conversely to challenge?

7) What does it say about *us* when we are reluctant to write a minimum number of practical, principle-based rules, and to enforce them with equity?

There's a final point that I would make on a theme from Proverbs 22:6. It says, "*and when he is old he will not depart from it.*" *(Amplified Version)* If you have a family member or other person whom you love, who is outside of the Kingdom of God, please don't despair. As long as they are alive there is hope. They haven't "turned out" yet. They are still in process. If this is the only thing you believe in what I've written, please believe that they *do* long to know God. Pray. Love. Accept. Try to understand. See the light in them even if it is barely visible. Speak blessing to them. Beg God to show you the roadblock in their heart and how you can be part of removing it—and to reveal any attitude, habit, or secret desire in your own life which could be handicapping them.

Grandparents who are in fellowship with God and in harmony with their family can have more impact than most realize. As long as we accept *any* responsibility before God for the life of those who follow us, we can have equivalent authority in the spiritual realm. We can influence, even from afar, but sometimes it will require humble soul-searching and even repentance on our part. I submit that our work is unfinished as long as we live and that we will never complete our responsibility toward our descendants.

Conclusion

To all, please take a new look at our youth, regardless of their age. They desperately need you in order to grow toward God. The church and the world need them. You need them. God will bless you and they will love you. What a deal!

And please believe this. Everyone wants to know God—even the heavily tattooed and pierced teens who are deep into drugs, alcohol, and sexual immorality. The degree to which they have strayed from normalcy indicates the depth of their search for "life." If we would love them more often, and weep for them instead of condemning and rejecting them, they would have a much greater chance of finding Him.

> ***May God make you a blessing*** *to the teens around you. May He allow you to see beyond their actions and give you insight into their hungry hearts. May you find incredible satisfaction in blessing and affirming their inner person, and joy in seeing it blossom into something beautiful. Something it might not have become were it not for you. And may they come to mind every time you break crackers in your soup!*

Yours, theirs, and His,

Ken Stoltzfus

Afterwords

A	RestCAT, Restless Child Analysis Tool
B	Public or Christian Education?
C	"God Help the Grownups!"
D	Potential Risks with Adoption
E	The Few as Adults
F	The Heart and Hand of God

A — RestCAT, Restless Child Analysis Tool

For reasons that are stated throughout this book, and probably more, we often misdiagnose a child when trying to understand their conduct.

Cars are more complex today than 20 years ago, and repair shops need current and sophisticated diagnostic tools to troubleshoot them when there's a problem. When was the last time you saw your auto mechanic place a screwdriver against an engine as it ran, and then put his ear against the tool to listen for the source of the problem?

The changing complexity of influences upon our children is at least equal to cars, and it makes our understanding of them increasingly challenging! To name a few factors, the influence of electronic gadgetry (if I named current ones the book would be obsolete before it was published), the erosion of moral standards, breakdown of family values, absence of masculine leadership in the home, and every kind of ungodliness imaginable (and some not) at our fingertips on the Internet—all work together to impact our children.

I propose that someone out there, possibly one working on a doctorate in teen development, create an analysis tool to help parents and institutional leaders, and possibly even the courts, better understand restless children.

The device would include a personality profile; an analysis of birth order factors and life experiences; home, church, and family cultures in terms of how they approach rules and their enforcement; and many other possible influences in the child's life, including the long list covered in Chapter 15.

My sense is that in spite of our human complexity, a tool of this nature could do a lot to help us understand restless teens to the degree that we could respond to them in a more constructive way. We'd be surprised, too, by how much our heart would reach toward them as we came to understand them better—and the effect of that would be amazing.

RestCAT could be developed to the point where many institutional leaders could use it, or taken to the level that one would need more training and even certification.

B — Public or Christian Education?

A Christian school with practical rules which are justly enforced in an environment of grace and mentoring is a real winner. Conversely, because of issues raised in this book, there are some student/school combinations where the student would be better off in a public setting.

And as you weigh Christian versus public education, please consider that the benefit of a Christian school to a particular student is based on the blending of the individual's personality and Christian walk, with various factors affecting local public education, the specific Christian school, and the student's home and church environments. There are legitimate arguments about the impact a Christian student can have in a public school, and vice versa. There are issues of educating in a sheltered atmosphere versus something more "real life." Yes, there are good reasons for Christian education and good reasons for public education!

Some of our nine grandchildren are in Christian

schools, others in public school. We know that each set of parents has their reasons and we support them equally in their choice. Based on several factors, we are just as optimistic about each of the nine grandkids regarding where they will be in their walk with God as they move on into life.

I hear Christians arguing and separating over Christian *versus* public education. Please don't do that. Because of the several factors addressed above, it is a subjective decision. Don't pit one against the other. Don't lift one up in a way that puts the other down. Bless, encourage, and pray for those who approach it differently than you, and work together for the welfare of our youth. Let's drop the word *versus* and use the words "public *or* Christian education!"

I respect home-schooling very much but have not mentioned it previously because it wasn't at the core of my concerns, except as it relates to the individual's home life and church experience. The principles of rules, authority, and mentoring apply to public schools as well, but our expectations would often be different from what we ought to be able to look for in a Christian school.

C — "God Help the Grownups!"

I see a host of individuals around me (mostly guys) in their 30s to 50s who are still struggling to find themselves in relationship to God. I know their hearts and their deep desire to do the right thing—to be more godly in general, and a better husband and daddy. They take a step forward, and then too often one or two backwards. I respect them so much and it's agonizing for me to see their struggle.

These are good men. *Very* good men. And some of the most "real" and delightful people you will ever meet. But they were severely wounded as teens at the hands of legalistic parents and other authorities, and they've never gotten beyond that definition of God. (They are further handicapped by the church's insistence that expressive, emotional, feminine spirituality defines true spirituality for all, but that's another discussion!)

Moving to my own generation, the realization of how many senior adults have experienced a diminished life decade after decade for the same reasons pains me deeply.

In either case, if that is you it makes me so sad to think of all the joy you have missed. You are fearfully and wonderfully made. You are precious in the eyes of God. He loves you very much and has been waiting all these years to flood your soul with value, meaning, and purpose. He is *not* the god who was communicated to you so many years ago.

Contrary to what we may have been taught about humility in conservative circles, there is a certain way in which we need to believe in ourselves if we are to be whole. By that I mean that we need to believe that "Even I" was carefully crafted by the hand of God, for His glory and our own joy! Read and personalize Psalm 139:13-16. Our greatest beauty is in being the distinct, unique person God wants us to be. One of our most humble expressions of surrender to God is to like being the person He created! Wow!! Be that! For Him! For yourself! For those you love! And for those around you who need to see *Him*, in a new you!

If you have believed the lies that others told you about your worth and beauty as a person, renounce them. Stand up, embrace the truth of who you are in God, and crush those lies under your foot. Maybe that would make you a new kind of "foot-stomping Christian." Ha!

God is very different from what may have been modeled for you "back then." He loves you for the person you are. After all, He formed your inner parts with His own hands! His love for you, yes, *you*, in spite of the past, is immeasurable. His mercy and kindness are unexaggeratable. He is waiting, ready to touch you and to become more to you than you ever dared to imagine.

If you are bitter about your upbringing, please forgive your parents, school administrators, church leaders, or others for their poor example or crushing expectations. They may have messed up, but they probably did the best they could with what they had. If you can't fully *forgive* right now, at least respect yourself and the "person" God has placed within you enough to "let it go." Trust the justice of God to take care of it for you according to the truth of Romans 12:19, or even vv14-19. They have probably already paid a terrible price for their sin against you.

It's time to move on with your life even at this hour! Ask God to help you rise to new levels in becoming what He intended you to be. Because of His persistent and abundant love and power it's never too late to start. It will look different now than when you were a teen, but the core person can still be revived, expressed, and enjoyed.

If you have unrighteous anger about the past, you can ask God to help it become righteous anger that is

Afterwords

expressed in an informed, constructive way in support of today's teens who are facing what you experienced back then!

Please consider this too. Regardless of the past, your present diminished life may be more of your own choosing than you realize. Too many years have gone by to hold others responsible. It's time for change and you can do it with God's help!!

One of my highest hopes is that God would use this book to draw some close to Himself who haven't known that blessing for most of their life. Maybe you or someone you know and love.

D — Potential Risks with Adoption

Adoption is one of life's purest expressions of the heart of Jesus. Opening one's heart, home—and yes, entire life to a child who might otherwise have little hope is amazingly close in spirit to what God did in bringing us back into relationship with Himself.

We know, however, that in many cases children were available for adoption only because they were unwanted by the birth parents or because of abuse or trauma in the home or their larger environment. There are exceptions, but this is often true.

It is widely accepted that a child experiences acceptance and rejection even while in the womb. And most certainly they do after birth. An infant is impacted by words of love or disdain because there is a spirit dimension to our words and attitudes. Words, and the way in which they are spoken, are not just sounds, they are "message." If the impact of past rejection or trauma is not countered, it can affect the child for his or her whole life and cause unspeakable confusion, frustration, and guilt for adoptive parents.

I encourage such parents to intercede for their child in this regard. In a particular way fathers, because of their leadership responsibility and spiritual headship, have authority to renounce the power of negatives which the child has been subjected to in the past. And little does more than the words of a mother to soothe the spirit of a child. They are two voices, each impacting the child in their own special way.

Adoptive parents have spiritual authority. You're *not* at the mercy of evil which was done against your child. Let righteous anger toward that evil rise up to empower and embolden you in defense of your child. Speak words of acceptance, life, peace, wholeness, and security—building a hedge of protection around them. And do it often.

It seems to me that there is something very special about going into a child's bedroom and praying over them while they are asleep, whether adopted or natural children. Without overstating it, we live in a spirit world. Parents can go individually or together. Kneel beside the child's bed, or stand alongside and raise your hand over them and do your work. Don't be surprised if God gives you an impression of a past violation against your child, so you can renounce and counter it. And we can speak blessing over them in our devotional time, when we send them off to school, and even in giving thanks for our food.

It is likely that if we live in an awareness of a child's possible need in this regard, that we will be more alert to symptoms of the pain of their past and can respond with various expressions of love, acceptance, and security as they grow up.

E — The Few as Adults

Here are some observations on experiences The Few will predictably have as they move through life as an adult. Obviously these are generalities, and individuals will see them played out in various ways and to various degrees in their own life.

- They will have many suggestions and ideas in the workplace. The way in which questions are asked and suggestions are given has a lot to do with how they are received. The time, place, attitude, and tone of voice affect how others will hear them, and they are responsible for that. A strategy I have used in relating to a strong leader is this. When I have a suggestion, and especially something confrontational, I'll go at what seems to be an appropriate time, say briefly what I have to say, in a tone of voice that communicates an option and not a mandate, and move on. I don't require a response. Most good leaders don't make fast decisions but will listen to sound advice. If what I say is worth receiving, they will probably process and accept it and all is fine. They might even accept my idea and take personal credit for it, and I'm okay with that too. Regardless, I've said my thing and I'm usually satisfied with that. It's more important for me to have my say than to have my way, although that's something I've had to grow into over the years.
- Regardless of the above, people may interpret their questions and ideas as a personal rebuff of their own

ideas, when they weren't intended that way. They were simply meant as a possible way for us all to do better.

- It will be very difficult for The Few to give leadership in a stagnant institution. A pastor who spends much of his time thinking outside of the box will face serious challenges in shepherding a flock that is satisfied with tradition. If they are asked to give leadership in an institution, they need to evaluate the situation realistically.

- Many institutions really don't want to change, and at least in some cases The Few will need to function on the outer edge of organizational power circles. Sometimes leaders *do* recognize the need for the institution to be different, and they would say that, but they are unwilling to pay the price of change in order to be different! Or present leaders may feel that doing things in a new way would be an indictment upon the past, when usually it isn't. More than others, outward-looking people will have to patiently earn the right to be heard. On the other hand, sometimes their being ostracized will embolden them: "Well, I'm already pushed out here and I have nothing to lose, so I might as well go for it." If the institution would respect them and give them an ear, it would soften their spirit and all would benefit.

- Most often it is The Few who are invited to restructure a weak or failing enterprise or institution. However, they need to know before going in that they can get bruised. It can be sort of like entering a war zone, and even more so in Christian institutions than in the business sector. Take the situation of an overseas mission with a 25-year history—but an ineffective administrative structure. Their free-wheeling culture had become like a mountain between them and the more professional management style they wanted. It is very possible that because of internal politics and vested interests in "the way we always did it," the first man in will be able to break the mountain into boulders but won't survive in leadership to crush it into stone for a new roadbed. Someone else will need to finish the job. It's good to know in advance that it's a risky assignment. It is also rewarding. Sometimes success is more in having done what God set before us to do than in results as we usually like to measure them.

F — The Heart and Hand of God

Here are some key Scriptures which convey the truth of the heart and hand of God on behalf of His own. Our "enemy" is Satan the deceiver, and his half-truths and lies which have so captured the mind and heart of humanity outside of the rule of Christ. More than we want to admit, the "problems" we have with teens are because of the measure to which he has also infiltrated the church, including us adults. I'd encourage you to do some personal study in these scriptures and ask God to confirm whether or not they apply to your relationship with youth.

<u>Joshua 23:10</u>
One of you routs a thousand, because the LORD your God fights for you, just as he promised.

<u>I Samuel 17:47</u>
All those gathered here will know that it is not by sword or spear that the LORD saves; for the battle is the LORD's, and he will give all of you into our hands.

Afterwords

II Chronicles 14:11
Then Asa called to the LORD his God and said, "LORD, there is no one like you to help the powerless against the mighty. Help us, O LORD our God, for we rely on you, and in your name we have come against this vast army. O LORD, you are our God; do not let man prevail against you.

Deuteronomy 20:1-4
Judges 4:14-16
II Chronicles 20
II Chronicles 32:6-8
Job 40:6-16
Psalm 1
Psalm 2
Psalm 3
Psalm 9
Psalm 16
Psalm 34
Psalm 35:10
Psalm 64
Psalm 73
Psalm 81:11-16
Psalm 85:8-13
Psalm 119:89-96 (read it all!)
Proverbs 1:20, 21 (wisdom speaks!)
Proverbs 8:1-3
Proverbs 9:1-6
Proverbs 11:5, 6
Proverbs 21:31
Isaiah 30:15-18
Lamentations 3:22-26
Hosea 10:13
Zephaniah 3:17-20
Matthew 5:1-16
I Peter 3:8-12

Has God changed since He had these Scriptures written for us? Is He at least equal to Satan in His ability to speak into the heart and minds of our youth and to influence them? And what does that say about God's part, and our part, in their nurture?

The Final Word

Scriptures referred to in the text, *New International Version*

Exodus 34:6, 7

6 And he passed in front of Moses, proclaiming, "The LORD, the LORD, the compassionate and gracious God, slow to anger, abounding in love and faithfulness, 7 maintaining love to thousands, and forgiving wickedness, rebellion and sin. Yet he does not leave the guilty unpunished; he punishes the children and their children for the sin of the fathers to the third and fourth generation."

Psalm 36:5-7

5 Your love, O LORD, reaches to the heavens, your faithfulness to the skies. 6 Your righteousness is like the mighty mountains, your justice like the great deep. O LORD, you preserve both man and beast. 7 How priceless is your unfailing love! Both high and low among men find refuge in the shadow of your wings.

Psalm 37:1-11

1 Do not fret because of evil men or be envious of those who do wrong; 2 for like the grass they will soon wither, like green plants they will soon die away. 3 Trust in the LORD and do good; dwell in the land and enjoy safe pasture. 4 Delight yourself in the LORD and he will give you the desires of your heart. 5 Commit your way to the LORD; trust in him and he will do this: 6 He will make your righteousness shine like the dawn, the justice of your cause like the noonday sun. 7 Be still before the LORD and wait patiently for him; do not fret when men succeed in their ways, when they carry out their wicked schemes. 8 Refrain from anger and turn from wrath; do not fret—it leads only to evil. 9 For evil men will be cut off, but those who hope in the LORD will inherit the land. 10

A little while, and the wicked will be no more; though you look for them, they will not be found. 11 But the meek will inherit the land and enjoy great peace.

Psalm 51:1
Have mercy on me, O God, according to your unfailing love; according to your great compassion blot out my transgressions.

Psalm 139:13-16
13 For you created my inmost being; you knit me together in my mother's womb. 14 I praise you because I am fearfully and wonderfully made; your works are wonderful, I know that full well. 15 My frame was not hidden from you when I was made in the secret place. When I was woven together in the depths of the earth, 16 your eyes saw my unformed body. All the days ordained for me were written in your book before one of them came to be.

Psalm 145:8-21
8 The LORD is gracious and compassionate, slow to anger and rich in love. 9 The LORD is good to all; he has compassion on all he has made. 10 All you have made will praise you, O LORD; your saints will extol you. 11 They will tell of the glory of your kingdom and speak of your might, 12 so that all men may know of your mighty acts and the glorious splendor of your kingdom. 13 Your kingdom is an everlasting kingdom, and your dominion endures through all generations. The LORD is faithful to all his promises and loving toward all he has made. 14 The LORD upholds all those who fall and lifts up all who are bowed down. 15 The eyes of all look to you, and you give them their food at the proper time. 16 You open your hand and satisfy the desires of every living thing. 17 The LORD is righteous in all his ways and loving toward all he has made. 18 The LORD is near to

all who call on him, to all who call on him in truth. 19 He fulfills the desires of those who fear him; he hears their cry and saves them. 20 The LORD watches over all who love him, but all the wicked he will destroy. 21 My mouth will speak in praise of the LORD. Let every creature praise his holy name for ever and ever.

Proverbs 1:7
The fear of the LORD is the beginning of knowledge, but fools despise wisdom and discipline.

Jeremiah 9:24
but let him who boasts boast about this: that he understands and knows me, that I am the LORD, who exercises kindness, justice and righteousness on earth, for in these I delight," declares the LORD.

Mark 9:42
And if anyone causes one of these little ones who believe in me to sin, it would be better for him to be thrown into the sea with a large millstone tied around his neck.

Romans 8:28
And we know that in all things God works for the good of those who love him, who have been called according to his purpose.

Romans 12:14-19
14 Bless those who persecute you; bless and do not curse. 15 Rejoice with those who rejoice; mourn with those who mourn. 16 Live in harmony with one another. Do not be proud, but be willing to associate with people of low position. Do not be conceited. 17 Do not repay anyone evil for evil. Be careful to do what is right in the eyes of everybody. 18 If it is possible, as far as it depends on you, live at peace with everyone. 19 Do not take revenge, my friends, but leave room for God's wrath,

for it is written: "It is mine to avenge; I will repay," says the Lord.

II Corinthians 3:18
And we, who with unveiled faces all reflect the Lord's glory, are being transformed into his likeness with ever-increasing glory, which comes from the Lord, who is the Spirit.

Ephesians 6:1-4
1 Children, obey your parents in the Lord, for this is right. 2 "Honor your father and mother"—which is the first commandment with a promise—3 "that it may go well with you and that you may enjoy long life on the earth." 4 Fathers, do not exasperate your children; instead, bring them up in the training and instruction of the Lord.

Colossians 3:20, 21
20 Children, obey your parents in everything, for this pleases the Lord. 21 Fathers, do not embitter your children, or they will become discouraged.

James 2:13
because judgment without mercy will be shown to anyone who has not been merciful. Mercy triumphs over judgment!

Revelation 3:18-20
18 I counsel you to buy from me gold refined in the fire, so you can become rich; and white clothes to wear, so you can cover your shameful nakedness; and salve to put on your eyes, so you can see. 19 Those whom I love I rebuke and discipline. So be earnest, and repent. 20 Here I am! I stand at the door and knock. If anyone hears my voice and opens the door, I will come in and eat with him, and he with me.

If not available from your local supplier, additional books may be purchased wholesale or retail from:

May be purchased for $5 each, postpaid in the U.S.
Please mail check or money order to:

Ken Stoltzfus
P.O. Box 228, Kidron, OH 44636

RESTLESS TEENS may be read, and downloaded free at
www.john2031.com/books/rt/main.html

See www.john2031.com for more inspirational resources

You might be interested in visiting the author's
web site for pilots and aviation enthusiasts:
www.FlyingHigher.net